MW00938199

Practical Leadership

First Published 2015

ISBN-13: 978-1512311655
ISBN-10: 1512311650

## Practical:

*"of or concerned with the actual doing or use of something rather than with theory and ideas"*

## Leadership:

*"the action of leading a group of people or an organization, or the ability to do this"*

# Contents

# Foreword by Denis Orme

As we know, there are five primary leadership styles, and multiple ways leadership can be practiced according to situations, and the people you are working with.

Too few quasi-leaders or managers understand and practice *Engaging Leadership.*

During my years in business restructuring where conducting exit interviews (usually with those who had already left the business or organization) I heard over and over:

"I would have stayed with the company if I could see it was going somewhere AND if my manager {or leader} had cared about me and my career."

The practices on Engaging Leadership include:

*Aligning & Appreciating:*     Engaging Leaders get everyone focused on where the company is going, and how the team supports the vision.  By Appreciating, the Engaging Leader gets to know each person on his or her team, their talents, strengths, aspirations, and concerns.

*Listening & Learning:*     By Listening, the Engaging Leader is receptive to all points of view, even those that are different from his or her own.  By Learning, the Engaging Leader continues to grow, replenishing and revitalizing his or her self.

*Energizing & Empowering:*     By Energizing, the Engaging Leader activates the excitement of the Mission, tapping into the human desire for autonomy, for self-determination, and for self-mastery.  By Empowering, the Engaging leader galvanizes and authorizes the team to Execute, trusting that a well-trained team will use its resources wisely to reach high quality decisions and actions.

———  ——

In this book Derek has laid out sound practical advice and tips which I believe lay the foundation for you to move forward, and gain the engagement of your staff in building an effective and enduring organization.

*Of course theory is just the starting point.*

With practice, can any of us be as good a golfer as Tiger Woods once was?  Probably not, but practice will certainly improve our game.

So too it is with leadership.  Not many of us will become a truly charismatic leader, but with practice we can all become much more effective in our leadership role in order to build a sustainable, profitable organization where staffs are fully engaged.

Continue your journey towards excellence utilizing the principles laid out in Derek's new book.

---

Denis Orme – International business restructuring consultant, and author.  His books include "Lessons From Leadership Failures," "High-Performing Teams" and "Engaging Leadership."

# Practical leadership

There are so many works centred on the topic of leadership and management. There are lots of theories, templates and models you can use and be exposed to. Theories are sometimes difficult to convert into practice so for this book, the focus will be on practical things you can use and do to enhance your skills as a leader and improve the engagement of those you lead.

There are age old arguments around the relationship between Leadership and Management. Some people believe they are synonymous and others argue about the subtle differences. In order for us to understand the perspective of this book, please consider the following:

*Leaders lead people and managers manage tasks.*

No one wants to be managed or supervised. Those terms have the connotation that someone isn't capable of working without someone being there to ensure they work properly. People want to be inspired and motivated to work and perform well.

If you think you're a supervisor or a manager, consider changing your title to 'Leader'. It's more motivating than the other options out there.

Searching a book store or the internet for books and advice on leadership will bring a large amount of options. There are so many leadership concepts out there. There's probably not a lot of new stuff but a lot of people saying the same thing in a different way. So if you are reading any of it, there's probably some value in it. The important thing is to use what works for you and the only way to find out what works is to try something out. You won't know just by knowing something, you have to use it and see what happens. We're all different and so are the people we lead.

At times, even the stuff you know usually works won't work, so it's good to keep on learning and especially let other people make the mistakes. So what's new in this book? Well, my experience has shown me that books like this can hold a few great little nuggets and I promise this will be no exception. As you read through this book or take a look at the material as a reference guide, you will come across some principles you may have heard of and others that may be new to you. As with all reading, it's best to keep an open mind and be ready for those moments where that flash of inspiration comes to you and is applicable to you and your role right now.

You may have read books before and felt okay about what you've read. You may have even been moved to action and I hope at times, while reading this work that you will feel inspired to make changes and to act in the areas that are relevant for you right now.

You may even return to the book and find new pieces of information that you didn't notice before, because your circumstances may be different. You may be struggling with a difficult staff member this week and the next you may be struggling to keep your staff on track with an imminent change. So even if you read this book all the way through in one go, don't think that you're done, as parts of it will mean more at different times. And certainly don't ever think you've learned all there is to know about leadership because you won't. Situations change, people change and so do all of the factors surrounding them - work, life and all that makes up your world in each successive moment.

## *What is leadership?*

Leadership is about the passion, the motivation and desire to get something done. As a leader you will be wearing both the leader's hat and the manager's hat. It's part of your role to figure out which hat to wear on which occasion. There's no doubt that sometimes you will need to make sure processes are followed, work is completed and reports are done (managerial tasks) and there are other times when you will be helping your team get behind the vision, discover their values and need to draw on their strengths (leadership).

Consider even how your words are used in both speech and in writing and you will be able to identify whether they are leadership words or managerial words. You may notice the difference in the response you receive too. Consider your email subject lines for example. Is the subject a phrase that focuses on the task or on the passion to complete the task?

## The brain and leadership

We know that the brain is made of two halves, one of which focuses on the logical, functional aspects (the left side) and the other which focuses on the creative and imaginative side (the right side). It's the latter which you can tap into regarding inspiring through your leadership skills.

Stephen Covey refers to a group working in the forest. The leader is the one who is with the team helping them to cut down the trees. He is there to help them make the correct swing with the axe, ensuring that the head is sharp and that they are working well together. The manager is in a tower making sure they are cutting down the right forest. In this simple illustration, you can see that the leader is with the people. They are not removed, poring over some report sending instructions by memo. A leader is with the team observing, motivating, correcting where necessary and ensuring the right effort is exerted and the job completed.

When the ancient Greeks of Platea marched in unison in battle it was the job of the Paraclete at the end of the line to motivate the group as they marched forward. He held a long spear and walked with the line shouting words of encouragement. His role was to keep the troops from running away and he would offer statements of hope as they marched, often to certain death. The word Paraclete itself means 'Hope is near'. As a leader, you should be there to offer hope and help the team see that their goals are achievable, practical and that you'll help them achieve them.

Take a moment and write down a few leaders you admire. You could consider current or former heads of countries - like Winston Churchill, leaders in their fields of expertise past or present like Steve Jobs or those you may know personally. What is it you admire about them? What character traits do they exhibit? Are there some collective traits which you would like to emulate?

Think about yourself. What are some of the characteristics about you that make you a good leader? Are there areas for improvement?

**Tip:**  Leaders lead people and managers manage tasks.

## *Are you a good leader?*

Having staff and being a leader can be both rewarding and frustrating. If you find it rewarding you are either doing some things right or are just darn lucky. If you find it frustrating, you may just be unlucky or you could benefit from the following tips on how to motivate your staff and be a manager that staff will want to work for. Although the following ideas are not an exhaustive list, they are some of the fundamentals that can help to make a good leader.

### Acknowledge your staff

When a member of staff does a job well, make sure you notice it, and acknowledge her or him for it. Don't let the opportunity to praise a piece of good work go by. Be careful that you don't embarrass them as some people don't like public recognition and others do. Learn what type of praise each of your staff members prefer and treat them accordingly. Everyone likes a compliment and it can greatly improve motivation and morale to reinforce good behaviour by acknowledging it. If they stay a little late to finish something off, if they put some extra effort in or whatever it is, a simple thank you can be very effective.

### Never, ever humiliate anyone on your team

If you are annoyed with someone on your team, or they have done something wrong, make sure you keep your cool, especially in public. If you humiliate someone, he or she will hold a grudge against you, and their work will suffer too. Always deal with difficult situations in private. If you have to give corrective feedback to someone, ensure it is directly with them. Don't try and do it in a group.

### Create a culture where mistakes are okay

If you don't make mistakes, chances are you are not stretching yourself. If your staff members are allowed to feel that mistakes are part of reaching for new highs, rather than something to feel bad about, or ashamed of, then they will take more risks on your behalf. In some cases, mistakes do need to be avoided but if you expect your staff to think for themselves or try out new things and stretch themselves a bit - they may fall short of your expectation but at least they'll be trying. Help them understand that making a mistake may mean they need to fix it and making the same mistake repeatedly is not acceptable.

### Remember personal details

Take time to get to know your staff; who they are, who and what is important in their lives, etc. Be interested in them as people, not just as workers. People will be more motivated to please you when they feel personally connected. Try to remember the small details. Listen to them. Ask them about their weekend, their plans etc. If they know you care there'll be no stopping them.

### Don't hide behind your position

Be human and friendly with your staff – that way you will all be able to support and encourage each other when things are tough. It's okay if you don't agree with everything from the top. It's okay if you're struggling with things too. If you communicate well and share frustrations but show how you are trying to support management as well, they'll see you're human.

### Be approachable

Allow your staff to feel that they can come and talk to you about sensitive issues, about inside – and outside – work difficulties, and that you will respect them, and not hold what they share against them. This means that you actually make time for them and not just say that you are there for them.

## Admit your mistakes

If you get it wrong, say so. Managers don't have to be infallible! Your staff will respect you more if you are able to admit your mistakes, and then set about sorting out a solution. An honest, no excuses apology or admission of a mistake is very powerful. If you cover everything up, they'll know and you'll lose their trust. If you can show that it's okay to take responsibility and how you fix it, then they will respect you for it. Use words like, "I'm sorry" and "I was wrong" and do so without fake humility.

## Be honest

If you want communication to be effective, you need to be real about it. Don't try and cover up information so people have to sift through and work out what is factual and what is a spin on the situation. Whether things are going well or not, honesty builds trust with your team. Also, don't put on an act. You don't have to try to be someone you're not. Your people will know when you are not being authentic.

## Listen in such a way that your employees will talk to you

Often people feel afraid of, or intimidated by, management. Make sure you show people that you are willing to listen to what they have to say, that they are important and worthy of your time.

## Be proactive

Be quick to head off any rumours. Share bad news in a timely way and give clear concise direction to your team. If something doesn't look right, it probably isn't so challenge the situation and don't be afraid to set things straight early on.

**Be clear in your requests**

It is your responsibility to ensure that people understand your requests – so communicate clearly, and ask if people have understood what you are asking for. Many hours of wasted work and effort can be spent because a leader hasn't been clear in their requests. To be a great communicator means to speak directly about things and avoid being ambiguous. Confirm their understanding so you know they are going to do what you want done. I will explain more on setting clear expectations later.

**Treat everyone respectfully and courteously at all times**

Particularly when there is a problem! Everyone who works for you is a valuable human being who deserves respect. A manager is only as good as how she or he treats the people on her or his team.

Being a good leader takes effort and consistency.

> **Tip:**    Don't forget the little things. Remember personal details, admit your mistakes, share the credit.

# What do you focus on as a leader?

There are many areas to focus on and sometimes this means that you will ironically lose focus. Consider what will be your critical success factors – those things you will be measured on by your superiors. These measures then will lead into critical activities.

Consider the coach of a basketball team. It's obvious they are watching both the scoreboard and the game. If they just watched the scoreboard they may miss vital information about how the game is being played. The team may be performing brilliantly and being just unlucky and yet the coach could change everything in the hope that the change could change the score.

Conversely, if the coach just watched the game, he may miss the fact that time is ticking away or that they need a change of tactic to get a different result.

In another example, consider the Olympic swimmer. They themselves are aware of what is happening in the water. They feel the drag, their breathing, any pains or strains on their muscles and yet the coach who is walking (or if they're really fast, running) alongside them in the pool has a different set of perspectives. They see the stroke, the amount of water splashing, their split times and a host of other things. It's combining the two perspectives that gives the greatest understanding of how to improve and maximise performance.

As a leader, you can't just rely on statistics and data. Neither can you ignore those facts. You need to look at the statistics and observe the performance. You should also get a view from the team members – the ones actually doing the work. What do they think is happening? They all go together and seeing them all in perspective and hand in hand puts you in a better place to make decisions.

# Critical activities

No matter what your role is, there will be core activities that you must focus on that will provide you with the results you need to achieve. If you're not sure what those activities are, make a list of the things you feel you need to accomplish in a month. For each of those activities on the list, link it through to a key measure or KPI (key performance indicator) that you are measured on in your role. Those activities that lead directly to a KPI or key measure that you have responsibility for are the critical activities you must do. Don't discount areas though that you find difficult to link through to the measures. For example, coaching your team may not be a direct measure you are given as a KPI but if you don't coach them, then their performance is likely to drop off or not improve. Believe the fact that whatever your team are measured on, that's where their focus will be so long as there are consequences in place for poor or non-performance.

There are four areas you can focus on as a leader to help your team achieve and perform well, namely: Give direction, coach, monitor and recognise.

### Give direction

This means that you are talking to your team regularly and frequently about what is happening, targets, goals, performance and about improvements that can be made. People want to be kept informed and clear, open communication falls under this vital component of a leader's responsibility. Tell people what's going on and help them have no doubt as to what they need to do and how it fits in the bigger picture.

### Coach

Coaching is an essential component of leading and allows you to reinforce desired behaviours and embed them as normal into the team. Remember that good coaches aren't just watching the scoreboard – they watch the game as well. Some days the scoreboard just won't reflect the effort and the performance. You need to watch both! This means that you need to observe your team members in action and provide effective feedback on the behaviours you see. Coaching can be rewarding for both you and your team members. Learn good coaching skills as it will have the biggest impact on your team.

### Monitor

You need to be able to track the progress of your team. Be careful here though and monitor only those areas that are really important. Remember that what we measure we focus on. Review what you're measuring regularly. If you don't know why you are measuring something find out why the measure is there in the first place. If nobody knows, it's probably not worth measuring. If it's not having an impact on the business or the team, why bother? When performance is measured, performance increases. When it's reported on, the rate of improvement actually accelerates, so make sure you report back on those measures.

### Recognise

People like to receive recognition. It doesn't matter if they are just doing their job - reinforce the performance by recognising it. Make sure though that however you choose to recognise someone, you do so in a way that's desired by the recipient. Use recognition early when you are trying to instil new behaviours as it will encourage the continuation of those behaviours. Ensure that you are sincere and avoid overdoing it as it will become diluted. Consider recognition when people consistently perform at a high standard, when they exceed your expectations, go above and beyond, or when you feel they need a bit more motivation.

## The Pygmalion effect

Named after the Greek myth of the sculptor named Pygmalion who fell in love with a statue he carved, this effect is that the greater the expectation placed upon people, the better they perform. There is an opposite effect called the Golem effect named after a clay creature given life in Jewish mythology. The Golem effect is essentially that the lower the expectation placed upon people, the poorer their performance is likely to be.

The Pygmalion Effect was described in the Harvard Business review in 1988 by J. Sterling Livingston as the following: "The way managers treat their subordinates is subtly influenced by what they expect of them". Every leader has expectations of the people who report to him or her. These expectations are communicated either consciously or unconsciously and people will pick up on them. People will then perform in ways that are consistent with the expectations they have picked up from their supervisor.

It's really a self-fulfilling prophecy then for people as they start to act the way you, as their leader, expect them to act. This can be very positive as staff members begin to excel in response to their leader's message that they are capable of success and are indeed capable of succeeding. A leader can, however, get the opposite effect by not treating all employees the same or by failing to praise someone where it is due.

A leader can extend the effect when they hold positive expectations of their staff. Just holding those positive expectations means they will naturally help improve the self-esteem of their people, and individuals in turn believe in themselves and their performance rises to meet their own expectations.

If someone believes they are capable of achieving a high standard, they are likely to internalise that positive label and excel in their role. Those that are constantly reminded of how useless they are, tend to lose ambition and provide a low standard of achievement.

As a leader, much of this is in your hands. You can certainly impact on the performance and motivation of an individual by your approach and the words you use.

Consider ways you can help your team members deserve greater expectations. For example:

- Relate to them the times when they have excelled
- Remind them of their capability to achieve
- Express your faith in them as a team
- Provide them with the tools to accomplish their tasks
- Ensure they have proper training and opportunities to practice
- Keep the communication positive
- Help them see the vision of their roles and the place it plays in the overall strategy

Just as the label a team member is constantly associated with is a good measure of their likely productivity levels, so is their level of engagement. We will discuss this next.

> **Tip:** A good coach or leader watches both the scoreboard and the game. One of the two is not enough to understand what exactly is going on.

# *Employee engagement?*

Employee engagement is a workplace approach designed to ensure that employees are committed to their organisation's goals and values, are motivated to contribute to organisational success, and at the same time are able to enhance their own sense of well-being. After a 2 year Gallup study around employee engagement in 140 countries, it was discovered that only around 13% of employees were actively engaged, 63% were not engaged and 24% were actively disengaged. (see Gallup poll 2011-2012 at Gallup.com)

## Maslow's theory of employee engagement

Abraham Maslow's theory of employee engagement is based on his Hierarchy of Needs model. The first level is around **survival**. These are employees who are actively disengaged and only at work for the money. **Security** motivates the next level up the scale. Again, these people are not engaged but enjoy the fact that they have some security in the role. Following on from the need to survive and feel secure is the need to **belong**. The being part of something is a driver that helps people be engaged. Sometimes people will say something like, "I love my job because of the people". Engagement grows further when people understand that what they do is **important**. If their work is helping to contribute and achieving, it naturally raises engagement. Finally, someone that is highly engaged looks for opportunities to help others to do their best too. They look for opportunities to develop themselves further and this is a level of **self-actualization**.

The UK government put some energy into identifying whether engagement made a difference and what helps it. In association with the organisation: www.engageforsuccess.org the result showed four main enablers which are highlighted through the management teams.

## Four Enablers

There are four basic enablers that great organisations use to help improve engagement with employees as follows:

**A Strategic Narrative**. This is the ability a leader has to be able to tell the story of the organisation: where we have come, where we are now and where we are going. Helping the teams understand and buy-in to the vision of the organisation creates a desire to be part of the whole. Help them understand the meaning of their role, which gives purpose to what they do. When an employee feels that what they do helps to achieve the vision, they are on board. There is a reference that when President John F. Kennedy visited NASA and saw a man with a broom in his hand, he asked him what his job was. The man replied, "My job Mr. President Sir is to help put a man on the moon."

**Engaging Managers**. There are three main things that engaging managers do. Firstly, they help the employee understand the scope of their role. They help them understand what success in their role looks like. Engaging managers also treat their staff as individuals. They are not an anonymous human resource but rather a human being. When they are treated this way, the organisation gets more out of them. The third thing managers do is to coach their people. Great managers are coaching on a weekly basis. Mostly it's about reinforcing positive behaviours and addressing any dysfunctional behaviour.

**Employee Voice**. Good organisations that have high engagement are good listeners. They give their employees a voice and let them talk across silos. They help them feel that their input is worthwhile. If something is about to go wrong in an organisation, someone somewhere always knows. If you want to be made aware of an impending issue, let your staff know that their input is welcomed and valid. If you see your people as part of the solution and not part of the problem, you will keep them well informed.

**Integrity**. Organisations should keep it real. What the organisation says they do, they should actually do it. They shouldn't pretend; there shouldn't be a gap between how you say you are and how you actually are. There needs to be a high level of trust. Integrity in this case is about what the leaders in the organisation say and what they actually do. If they match, then there is integrity. If they don't then employee engagement starts to suffer.

If you are struggling with employee engagement, look at these four enablers for ideas about starting the process of what you need to do. Of course, there does need to be a level of consistency throughout the organisation for it to really stick, so try holding senior managers accountable for their role in this. After all, their salaries are dependent on being employed too and if productivity levels are not what they should be, it's likely down to lower staff engagement levels. One final thought on engagement, the Gallup poll also stated that 20% of managers / leaders were engaged. That leaves 80% of managers / leaders in a state of non-engagement. If managers / leaders aren't there yet, how can we expect the staff to be?

**Tip:** Understand what the four enablers of engagement are and ensure you have a handle on them as applied to your organisation.

— —

# Influencing others

The ability to influence others is a core leadership skill. Influencing is quite like persuasion, in that you are helping people see things as you do. It is however, not like manipulation, where you try and get people to change their ideas or behaviours to suit your gain alone. There are some core areas you can work on which will help you build your influencing skills in a practical way.

Firstly, know what you want and believe that you can get it. This all starts from the inside. Being clear about our sense of purpose and goals is the first step.

Credibility is something that other people perceive about us. It is the quality, capability or power to elicit belief. Our credibility with someone comes from three things – the relationship we have with them, how they perceive our expertise and what has happened in the past.

Being trustworthy is a fundamental element of influence. The most influential people are those who operate from values such as truth, trust and integrity and use those values with the intent to benefit not just themselves but the people around them as well. If you have recommended something in the past that has not worked, don't avoid this. Be open in your communication. Be ready with answers about past misses. If someone trusts you, they are already most of the way there.

We are unlikely to influence someone from our own point of view. We need to be able to step outside of our own perceptual position and explore someone else's view of the world.

Consider your ability to develop an empathetic view of others. However self-aware, genuine and honest we are, the ability to get others to follow comes from our capacity to communicate effectively. Highly influential people are usually articulate, willing and able to listen and able to present their ideas with clarity and conviction.

Look at ways to be inspirational. Enthusiasm is infectious. We have all experienced how contagious negative emotion can be and it is equally true of positive energy. Inspiring others involves motivating and capturing their imagination. Martin Luther King used powerful imagery in his famous 'I have a dream' speech – the picture he painted and the feelings it evoked did far more to capture the imagination and influence others than a factual account would have done.

When you are trying to influence someone, focus on the other party. Try not to want anything yourself and look at things from the other party's perspective. What will be the benefit to them? What does the other party need? What are their expectations and interests? Ensure you give them time to explain these to you or do your research beforehand. This will develop some trust and show them that you are interested in them. When it comes to a proposal, you will be able to show them benefits that will be easy for them to understand and buy into.

Consider how you feel toward the other person and them to you. If you like someone, you will be able to focus on their needs more. If the other person likes you, you will find it easier to influence their decision. This is basic information but we often overlook the simple components that work well. Look for something in the other person you like and use that to help you in your communication.

Help with ownership. People get more attached to their own ideas. Part of your job in influencing is to help the other party feel like they have come up with the idea or suggestion themselves. Use questioning techniques to help them come to a solution themselves if you feel like they will respond better to their own ideas.

Try not to be so set on one thing that if that becomes impossible, all is lost. Sometimes, we are offered things when we aren't looking for them or aren't fighting for them. If you had your heart set on seeing a particular movie at the cinema but when you got there, all the seats were taken, do you complain and go home in a huff or do you look for an alternative movie to watch and still enjoy some time out? Consider other options prior to trying to influence others. Flexibility and a willingness to be influenced are also traits that are evident in most influential people.

Ensure you make sense. People may want to verify what you say or claim. Ensure that you have researched your ideas properly and have supporting information where possible and where necessary.

Avoid being hesitant and use positive language. Avoid words like "you know", "umm", "kind of", "I mean". Using words like these will mean people will be less likely to believe what you are saying. Instead of saying "You're wrong about this", say "That's true, however ...", "That's an excellent idea, but if we look more deeply ....." or "I agree with what you say but have you considered ....".

Compliment the other party. For example: "I see that you've done some great research into this". Even though they may realise this is being done, evidence shows that they will still warm to you and be more open to your proposals.

Mirror the other person's mannerisms (e.g. hand and body movements). People you mirror subconsciously feel more empathy with you. A study at INSEAD Business School found that 67% of sellers who used mirroring achieved a sale compared to 12% who did not. However, it can be very embarrassing if the other person detects conscious mirroring so it must be very subtle. You need to leave a delay of between two and four seconds before the mirroring action.

Try to remember the names of everyone you meet. It shows that you are treating them as an individual. Jennifer Chatman of USC, Berkeley developed some experiments to try and find out if there was a point at which flattery became ineffective. She found out there wasn't one.

You may not consider yourself a good influencer. You can learn. A lot of it comes from being confident. You build confidence through having knowledge and through practice.

> **Tip:**  Being influential helps when you develop a feeling of trustworthiness and credibility. Own up when things don't work out but have answers as to why.

—— ——

# Goal setting

Setting goals is a great way to help your team see that they are achieving and it helps to get the work done. You may already have a set number of KPIs (Key performance indicators). These are measures that are in place to help management see that things are on the right track and that the critical activities are being focused on.

One of the errors some leaders make is to focus on the wrong stuff. They may be busy alright but in the wrong areas or in doing things that don't really matter that much or that don't have a massive impact on the team or the business. Take reports for example. They're necessary but some people spend most of their time wrapped up in doing administration rather than leading the people. A leader's job is to be with the team and help them to achieve. You can't do that effectively from behind a desk.

Some leaders say they know what's going on because they can see their team from where they're sitting. I challenge you to know what is actually going on in those conversations with customers from your desk. You need to watch, observe, listen and engage with your team to fully understand what is happening. If you lead a team of sales people who are out on the road, you can't possibly know what is going on unless you spend time with them. Go with them to occasional meetings and find out how they operate.

So, in order to help stretch your team members, help them to set meaningful and achievable goals. Consider using the SMART goal method:

- Specific
- Measurable
- Agreed
- Realistic
- Time-bound

Be specific in what it is you want them to achieve. You can't say for example that you want them to improve their performance. It just isn't specific and you will then be in an argument about what improvement looks like. So when you set goals and want to be specific, describe what it is you want them to achieve.

In fact guide them to come up with the goal where possible. If they decide upon it, they will be more likely to want to achieve it. You may ask, "How many calls do you think you can make this week?" This gives them the opportunity to come up with the number. Now if it's too low, you may need to coach them a bit around being realistic, stretching, being sensible etc but help them come up with it. Once you have the goal, just make sure it is specific and then measurable. Will you be able to actually measure that they have achieved it when it is complete.

Do not impose goals on your team. If they don't own the goal, they will feel much less inclined to go for it. This is the 'agreed' part of the acronym.

Goals should be realistic and achievable. There's no point setting a goal so high that it's impossible to achieve. Some people think that if you set goals really high, you may still get some kind of achievement but if you never actually attain goals, they will always be looked on as 'out of reach' and people will never believe they will be achievable.

Finally ensure that there is a timescale involved. People need to know when the deadline is. Without a timeframe, a goal will remain open-ended forever.

The SMART goal provides some boundaries for people to stay inside of. People need boundaries but they don't want rules to be so rigid that there is no room for individuality or interpretation.

When you have your goals set with your team, let them know what the follow up plan is. Let them know when and how they will need to report back to you. If there is no accountability at the end, or a goal, then they may never achieve it and you may never know either way.

No accountability means people will see no value in the goal. Hold people accountable and give them all the support they need to get it accomplished. Don't strangle them with leadership though. Give them space. In fact, talk to them about how they would like you involved. Do they want regular catch ups or not. Do they want you to comment on how they are doing? These things are personal preferences. You may need to vary things up for different people.

## *The GROW model*

You could consider using the GROW model which is another coaching technique. The GROW model or technique was developed in the UK and used extensively in the 1980s and 1990s.

The four stages are:

- Goal
- Reality
- Options / Obstacles
- Way forward

The Goal is the end point - where you need to be at the end. This is why it needs to be SMART so there is no ambiguity about what is to be achieved, by when.

The Reality is the gap between the current situation and where the goal is. This is best looked at as a self-assessment from the team member. This needs to be real and clear. You may need to help them understand exactly what the gap is. You may like to help set a number of steps in place to be achieved on the way to the goal. It's easier to achieve small steps than one huge one.

Options can then be discussed to look at ways to overcome any obstacles. Discuss and offer options that could be considered. This is a great place to ask powerful questions like, "What do you think you will need to change to actually achieve this goal?"

The Way Forward is to decide upon the next steps, identify what support is needed and include review dates and possibilities. Ensure you end positively.

> **Tip:**   Ensure that each goal you set comes with accountability. Work on having your team member set the goal. Your job is to guide them in ensuring it is realistic.

— —

# Motivating your staff

Admit it, some days motivating your staff is like pushing rope! It's that silver bullet of leadership – keeping your staff motivated on a sustained basis. There are short term fixes like buying them all ice creams on a hot day or longer term tricks like reward and recognition schemes. We've all seen the survey results about what motivates people to come to work, but what gets them to do their work once they get there? The three big motivators can be summed up as:

- The Need to Achieve
- The Craving to Contribute
- The Burn to Learn

If you're stuck for motivational ideas – try to link back to one of these and you won't go wrong. Here are some great ways to keep your staff motivated:

## Goal setting

Do you and your staff have a clear idea of what it is you need to achieve, when you need to achieve it and how? Do you have one goal for the company or do individuals have their individual goals to meet to help achieve the company goals? Is the goal's progress fed back to the team on a regular and constructive basis? Do they feel like they are an integral part of the organisation? People want to feel like they are contributing and that their work is meaningful. Let them know how their efforts impact the big picture.

## Sense of achievement / positive reinforcement

Catch people doing things right instead of always waiting for them to make a mistake. A simple but powerful statement such as "You did a great job today" or "Thanks for that" go a long way and cost nothing. Everyone likes personal recognition. Do not engage in empty praise. Always make it meaningful.

## Reachable / attainable targets

Are targets set at a realistic and achievable level – high enough to stretch staff to find levels within themselves but not too high or too distant for people to give up? If targets are too easy, staff will not stretch themselves. Find the balance and watch the difference.

## External versus internal stimuli

What is the balance between staff self-motivation and the drive to get things done and the need to constantly push or punish staff into doing the same things? External motivation is short lived, whereas internal motivation remains – even when you are not there. Do you know, I mean really know, what motivates your staff? If not, then take time to find out - it will pay dividends in the long term.

## Honesty

Do not mislead or lie to your staff. People react better to direct honesty. Even if it is a hard call, make it, they will appreciate your honesty. If you make a mistake, own up to it. Never criticise in public.

## Support

Do they have the support they need? Do they get the mentoring and coaching they may require to help them when they need it?

## Direction / Vision

Does your team have crystal clear vision of where the company is going and why? Vision statements on the walls are not enough. Your company vision needs to be constantly in focus –

talked about, planned, measured and refocused. If people buy into your vision for themselves, the company will become an exciting place to work.

For people to be able to do something well, they need to have three things:

1.  Knowledge of what to do
2.  Skills for performing the task
3.  A desire to do it

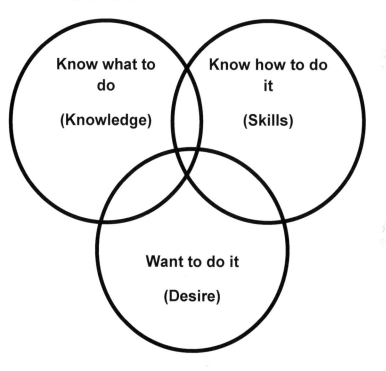

It's no good just having one or two of those things – all three are needed in order to get the best result.

When you're motivated to do something, you will be much more likely to accomplish it faster and more efficiently than when you're not. Motivation is our driving force. We are all motivated by different things and when we find ourselves 'in flow' where the time just whizzes by, we know that we are motivated in doing what we are doing.

Unless the person being coached wants to change or listen to you, it's unlikely that anything will change at all. The person needs to have the desire to change. People try all sorts of methods to motivate staff members, and coaching is no different. What we really want is for the coachee to want to change their behaviour or to want to do what it is we are recommending. If we take the various motivation options, we could put them into a simple matrix:

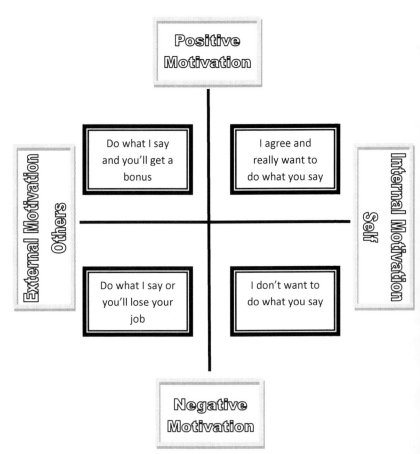

Basically, unless the person wants to change or do what's required, the likelihood is that they won't! Using negative motivation (for example - do it or you're fired!) may only gain a short term positive response. Like any external motivation, once the external motivation has gone, so has the desire. Even with positive motivation – if it's externally pushed (for example - do it and you'll get a prize) will mean that when the prize is no longer there, the desire has gone too. You'll have to keep providing prizes to keep up the motivation and the chances are you'll have to start increasing the perceived value of the prizes to keep their interest. Oh, and by the way, their salary is not considered enough of a prize in most cases.

This motivation using positive and negative consequences is a fascinating topic and you may like to research a bit more. Try searching articles on 'Operant Conditioning' if you would like to know more.

### 'Why' not 'what'

The real winner for motivation is to help create an internal desire to perform the task, make the change or act in the way you want them to. Now that's easier said than done but there are some key principles you can use in order to impact on this result. Firstly, understand what drives the individual in the first place. What pushes their buttons? What are their interests? The more you know about them, the easier it will be to tie in a motivator to their role or task.

As an example, one person – we'll call her Mary - was struggling to be motivated to do her role. She worked for a government department in a call centre. Her great love was opera singing. How on earth was the manager going to find a link to help motivate her to improve her interactions with callers? During the discussion, the manager started to focus on the 'WHY' rather than the 'WHAT'.

So often we spend our energies talking about what people like to do and what motivates rather than why we like to do it or why it motivates them. During this discussion, Mary explained that she loved the way she made people feel after performing opera. They felt better somehow, lifted and happier. Once the manager got this information, she was able to help Mary see that by doing her job well, she could also make people feel better, lifted and happier by dealing with their queries and helping them resolve any issues. That was it! That was all Mary needed to get going and perform. She had discovered a link between what motivated her and her job.

Getting this right will help you get buy-in from the individual. Buy-in means that you see the benefits and want to proceed with it 100%. It's more than supporting the idea and certainly more than accepting it. We all accept the price of petrol – because we pay it – but I don't think we all have buy-in for the price it is set at. We're not eagerly queuing up to fill our tanks the minute we see the needle dip just below full – we're more likely to drive to the near-limit of the tank before we grudgingly go to the petrol pumps. Support for something means that we will tell people it's a good idea. We see some benefits. We might pay a contribution to a cause because we support it but we might not be up at 4am to join in the protest march or do without the new TV and donate all the money.

It's not until we really get behind something – live and breathe it, see that it's the only way and drive ourselves there without the need for someone else - that we have buy-in. When the manager has left for the day, we continue on as normal because we are internally motivated to do so. We are not relying on the manager watching us to perform at our best.

> **Tip:** Remember that everyone wants to achieve, contribute and learn – these are the three basic motivators.

## *Motivation by appreciation*

Why do employees really leave companies? Most managers believe that their employees leave the companies they work for because of money. This is simply not true. A four year study conducted by a leading third-party exit interviewing firm in the United States found these results from thousands of interviews: 89% of managers believed that their employees left for more money and 11% for other reasons. It was quite the opposite in fact though: Only 12% cited money as the reason for leaving and 88% for reasons other than pay.

Most of the reasons given for leaving had some psychological base such as not feeling trusted or valued. In fact, many businesses are at risk of losing quality employees because they feel unappreciated or unvalued.

If supervisors and managers are unaware of this, they will focus more on the financial benefits. This is futile when the attitude of staff becomes one of, "They couldn't pay me enough to stay here!"

In addition to this, managers consistently report that the process of hiring and training new staff is one of the most disliked tasks they have, let's not forget the mammoth cost behind this task too.

A Gallup poll in the United States reported that 70% of people receive no praise or recognition in the workplace. There is a definite correlation between staff retention, staff engagement, job satisfaction and the appreciation that is shown them in the workplace. The level of satisfaction at work is significantly influenced by how appreciated staff feel by their managers and co-workers.

Companies spend vast amounts of money on reward and recognition programmes, whereas engaging in simple 'motivation by appreciation' techniques is inexpensive, personalised to the individual and goes far for employee confidence and output levels.

## Appreciation in the workplace

Following the very successful **'5 love languages'**, Gary Chapman teamed up with Paul White and worked through motivation by appreciation in the working environment. Their four year studies have led to amazing results and the principles have proved to be very popular within the business community.

In basic terms, people respond to appreciation being shown in 'their language of appreciation'.

We are all different and we respond to appreciation showed in different ways. The five main languages described are:

1. **Words of affirmation**
2. **Tangible gifts**
3. **Quality time**
4. **Acts of service**
5. **Appropriate Physical touch**

In terms of workplace appreciation, the physical touch language is more difficult to incorporate – purely because it could be misconstrued and that's why the addition of the word 'appropriate' is often added. However, a firm handshake or a 'high five' could work in those cases. More recently, physical touch as a language of appreciation is becoming more demonstrable. Sports teams for example are constantly using fist bumps, high fives and group hugs to bond. In one study, the winning team of a basketball competition were seen to have over 200 physical touches prior to the game – more than twice that of the other teams.

Understanding which language of appreciation each of your staff members respond to will help guide you on how to show appreciation to them.

Showing appreciation needs to be done in a sincere manner. If managers can learn to express sincere appreciation they may make the difference between success and failure for a business. Employees who feel valued will be more loyal to the business than those that don't.

## Do you appreciate your colleagues and staff?

Many people may feel that they do appreciate their co-workers and their staff and many will say they show it too. The real question is,

### 'Do your staff members _FEEL_ appreciated?'

We may feel like we show appreciation but if it is not in the way our staff want it, it may mean nothing.

For example, if a manager tells a staff member frequently that he appreciates all they do, he may feel he has shown appreciation. However, if that staff member could really do with some help sometimes, they may feel that the words are meaningless. If the manager really understood the staff member and helped them out with a task or two, the appreciation would be 'felt' by the staff member and register highly to them.

## Which language do I use?

You may understand your own language of appreciation but that may not be what each of your staff members need. In a lot of cases, leaders show appreciation in the way they observe others showing appreciation which is also missing the mark just as showing appreciation the way they like to be shown it does.

Truly understanding this concept can motivate your staff members to be more loyal and increase engagement and productivity without increases in salary or bonuses. Try to find out which way your staff members wish to be shown appreciation. It may surprise you and if you act on it, so may the results!

Dr Paul White who co-wrote the book 'Motivation by appreciation in the workplace' states: "Make sure your communication is personal and fitted to the individual rather than utilizing general communication. The key component to effective appreciation and encouragement is the sense by the recipient that you mean what you say and that you took time to think about them personally."

Dr. White's research found that a global "Thanks for a good job done" email to a wide range of people across the organisation actually generated a negative response from most team members, given the impersonal nature and perceived minimal effort completed. 'Speak the language' of the person of whom you are trying to encourage.

Dr. White indicates each of us has a primary and secondary language of appreciation, such as:

**Words of Affirmation:** *Words of recognition or affirmation from a supervisor*

**Quality Time:** *One-on-one quality time with leader*

**Acts of Service:** *Help from others on a project*

**Tangible Gifts:** *Receipt of a gift card to area shopping, events or restaurants*

**Appropriate Physical Touch:** *Strong handshake, high five or hand on the shoulder*

### Words of affirmation

Using words of affirmation is the way you can communicate a positive message to someone in the workplace. Using this type of language, you verbally affirm a positive characteristic about someone. They may be honest, kind, thoughtful, unselfish, hardworking or compassionate and we can positively affirm this to them by verbally recognizing these character traits.

You can also speak words of appreciation to people in what we observe people do. Basically, you can comment to the person about them doing a quality job or for exceeding expectations. Insincere and generic words of praise like "good job", "you are a good worker", "keep it up" etc do not encourage. These types of words are not words of appreciation in the workplace because they sound robotic. Instead, you should be specific about the task, behaviour, or quality that you see and appreciate. This is the only way to make your words have meaning.

**Speaking words of appreciation**

You can speak words of appreciation in the workplace in multiple ways, but it is important to consider what the receiver would prefer.

1. You can make it personal and speak to your colleague one-on-one.
2. You can praise your colleague in front of others (such as your colleague's supervisor, colleagues, clients, etc.)
3. You can provide written affirmations.
4. You can praise them in front of a larger audience and in a more formal manner (like at a dinner or awards ceremony).

In the book, 'The 5 languages of appreciation in the workplace', some examples of what people who were surveyed wanted included:

- Occasionally tell me, "Thanks for working hard."
- Write me an email and acknowledge when I have done a good job
- Acknowledge my effort on a project, in the presence of my colleague
- Tell others (when I am not around) about the good job I am doing
- Give me a specific compliment when I have done something well
- In my review, write a specific list of things you like about my work performance

- Praise me in private, not in front of others
- Write me a handwritten note of appreciation
- Give me encouragement after I handled a difficult situation
- Give our team a group compliment when we have done well.

## Quality Time

Some people will like you to spend quality time with them. This is a great way to show that you value their contributions at work. Some leaders interpret their employees' desire for quality time as an inappropriate desire to be their friend, or an effort to get on good terms with the boss in order to have an undue influence and receive favours. People who value others and who realize that their greatest and most important resource is people, don't think this way.

So where do you find the time to spend quality time at work? According to one study, workers can waste over 3 hours of the 8 hour workday. About 44% of employees spend time surfing the internet during work. Of those that surf the net, they waste about 18 hours per week doing so. By making better use of your time you can make time for quality time.

## What does quality time in the workplace look like?

Quality time does not mean just working close to your staff. It means giving the person your undivided attention. The appreciation language of quality time has several dialects: quality conversation, shared experiences, small group dialog, and working in close proximity.

Quality conversation requires you to be a good listener and some suggestions to improve in this area are to:

- Maintain eye contact
- Not multitask while listening,
- Listen for feelings and thoughts

- Affirm feelings even if you disagree with their conclusions
- Observe body language and ask for clarification when body language and words do not align
- Refuse to interrupt.

Research indicates that people listen for 17 seconds before interrupting.

'Shared experiences' is another dialect. This is the sharing of any experience whether it is directly work related (working on a project together) or something that happens outside of work (going to an event together). Men whose primary language of appreciation is quality time prefer shared experiences as an expression of appreciation.

Third, there is small group dialog. For those individuals who are not comfortable with just one-on-one dialog, then group dialog is best for them. Some employers hold regular small group chats or daily huddles and they have found that excellent ideas for improvements, come as a result of those sessions.

And finally, there is working in close proximity. In volunteer situations this is the most effective. Research indicates that volunteers have a greater sense of satisfaction when they believe that what they are doing makes a difference and when they feel that their contributions are recognized and valued as they work closely with others.

People whose preferred language of appreciation at work is quality time have suggested the following examples as ways for leaders to demonstrate this language:

- Go to lunch together to talk about business issues
- Go to lunch together just for fun
- Stop by, sit down in my office, and check in with me about how things are going.
- Take a walk together during the lunch hour
- Come "hang out" with the team at the end of the day
- Have an off-site retreat for the staff

- Get together to watch sporting events
- Go to dinner together with our spouses/significant others
- Give me a call occasionally, just to chat.

## Acts of Service

Acts of service in the workplace may not always be easy for a leader to perform and it is difficult to perform acts of service when the focus of work is to get ahead and achieve goals regardless of the impact that may have on others.

A true leader will see their role is to serve those they lead. In reviewing this language of appreciation, consider these important components to provide acts of service effectively:

- Make sure your own responsibilities are covered before volunteering to help others
- Ask before you help (if you dive in to help and they do not want it, it can create tension)
- Serve voluntarily (a supervisor should make a request instead of demand support for an individual who needs help)
- Check your attitude (make sure it is positive and cheerful)
- Do it their way (do things their way so that they can feel that it was done right)
- Complete what you start (but also communicate and work within the limits of your time)

## Tangible Gifts

This language may of course involve some expenditure but doesn't need to be expensive. The most important aspect of this and indeed of all of these languages of appreciation in the workplace, is that the thought must be genuine and in this language in particular, it is the thought that counts and not the amount of money that was spent.

Your staff and even colleagues will appreciate that someone took the time to notice one of their interests or hobbies. This gesture alone makes them feel that they are seen as people and not as a 'human resource'.

Thoughtless gifts - those gifts bought quickly in response to tradition or a feeling of obligation with no real personal investment of time or reflection, not only miss the mark but also communicate a negative message. As a leader, try to understand what your employees would appreciate as gifts. People often do not want things but want experiences, such as:

- Tickets to sporting events
- Gift cards to restaurants
- Tickets to cultural events
- Short vacations/retreats
- Certificates to a spa, for a manicure, a free round of golf
- Shopping money at the local mall
- Gift cards to a housewares store

## Appropriate Physical Touch

More of today's human resource professionals spend their time advising around sexual harassment issues, so suggesting physical touch as a method of showing appreciation needs to be carefully advised.

Touching, however is a very real human response. You may have noticed when someone gives bad news; they may often put their hand on a shoulder or take someone's hand.

A few areas you may consider if someone's language of appreciation is physical touch could be:

- A high five
- A handshake
- A hand on the shoulder
- A fist bump

It is important to know what your staff members want by way of appreciation. As previously mentioned, if we 'speak in the wrong language' we may do more harm than good or at least at best do no good at all.

Take the example of a manager always saying to one of their staff members that they do a great job. Even verbally appreciating the extra effort they have noticed them putting in. One day, the manager and the staff member are sitting opposite one another in an HR discussion and the staff member says she doesn't feel appreciated by her manager. The manager may say something like, "How can you say that? I am always telling you what a great job you do and how I appreciate your efforts." The staff member could respond with, "It doesn't do anything for me. What I could really do with is a helping hand once in a while."

Take time out to understand what your team members prefer when it comes to motivation by appreciation. If you get it right and are sincere it can go a long way to improving loyalty and motivation without costing you in financial terms.

As a rough guide, Dr Paul White has outlined the top ten easiest ways to show appreciation in the workplace as follows:

1. Give a verbal compliment (say "thanks for ..."; tell them, "I'm glad you are part of the team.")

2. Write an email ("I just wanted to let you know ...; "It is really helpful to me when you ....")

3. Stop by and see how your colleague is doing. Spend a few minutes just chatting and checking in on them.

4. Do something together with your co-worker (like eating together.)

5. Do a small task for someone spontaneously (hold open the door, offer to carry something.)

6. Stop by their workspace and see if they need any help getting something done.

7. Buy them coffee, a drink, a snack or dessert.

8. Get them a magazine related to an area of interest they have (sports, hobbies, a place they would like to visit.)

9. Give them a "high five" when they have completed a task (especially one that has been challenging or they have been working on a while).

10. Greet your colleague warmly, with a smile and a handshake. (Say something like "It's good to see you!"; "How is your day going?")

courtesy: www.drpaulwhite.com

**Tip:** Learn what language each of your staff members speak and ask yourself the question, "Do they FEEL appreciated?"

# Getting your team to work better together

Most leaders would like their teams to work together better at some point. Perhaps the team is new or the dynamics just aren't sitting right or maybe the team has never really functioned as well as it could. I'd like to suggest some ways that your team could understand each other better and work together more effectively.

## Communicating

Fundamentally the simplest area to look at is how the team is communicating. Having open and honest communication can take away the 'indirect language' that causes confusion and assumptions. As the leader, you should lead by example and ensure that what you say is clear and to the point. Encourage the type of communication with each other in the team to be the same. One simple test is to ask team members to make sure 'an exchange of understanding' has taken place. This means clarifying and checking understanding. It's not enough to say: "I sent you an email" or: "I told you about that". It's important to check that people both receive and understand the communication.

## Share preferences

Have the team members get in the habit of sharing their preferred way of dealing with work things. For example, if someone prefers to have time to think about a topic rather than be expected to share opinions on it at short notice encourage them to declare that preference. Some people get annoyed when people don't speak up at meetings when it just may be the person's preference to think things through. If people hate it when agendas aren't adhered to, learn to understand that preference. When team members are sensitive to other's preferences, they understand them and their point of view much better. Consider your team's preferences in organisational work habits, meetings, processes and communication areas especially. You could take five minutes at each team meeting to take turns for everyone to share a preference or two. These preferences can be explored well using the Team Management Index (TMP Profile).

## Express thanks & celebrate successes

Take time out to thank, enjoy and celebrate when things have gone well. Cultivate a culture of appreciation - even if it's for people doing their job. When an achievement is made which is out of the ordinary, take time to celebrate the achievement. If people feel appreciated, they are likely to respond better when you need them to push a bit further or stay a bit later. Showing appreciation, giving compliments and rewards all help to motivate people.

## Accountability

Establish a culture of accountability. If someone is not pulling their weight, you need to address it. Team members that work hard see when others aren't putting in the same effort. You need to show to the whole team that fairness is a principle you want to adopt. You can build trust faster in a team when you hold each team member accountable for their efforts and results. Consider consequences for non-performance or below par effort. Positive consequences for good performance should also be considered.

## Share responsibility

Help develop the team by sharing responsibility. Delegate some tasks to help develop skills. Challenge the team so they are given opportunities to grow and stretch. This means they may make mistakes - make sure that's okay and help them to learn and recover from them. If you don't allow mistakes people won't want to try new things because they'll be too afraid to. Remember that if you are looking for a promotion at some point, you want to have someone prepared to take over your role otherwise you may not get the chance.

> **Tip:** Work on having clear, transparent communication. Ensure that there is an exchange of understanding.

—  —

# Communication

It's the basis for how we interact with one another. We have some fantastic tools to help us communicate. These tools are not communication themselves. For example, talking and listening are tools for communicating but don't necessarily add up to communication. For example, if one person spoke in German and the other person didn't understand German – then they are not really communicating – even if the listener was concentrating on what the person was saying.

Communication is the **"exchange of understanding"**. It is the sharing of information where both parties understand one another. Tools to help in that exchange of understanding include:

- talking (through questioning and statements)
- listening
- paraphrasing
- body language

## *Listening skills*

To be a good coach, you need to be a good listener. Here are some of the poor listening skills areas to be aware of. Take a pen and mark a 'Yes' or a 'No' next to each one that best indicates your answer.

1. I anticipate what people will say next as they are speaking
2. I'm constantly judging the merit of what people say from the very first sentence
3. I discount what other people say if they don't agree with my opinions and values
4. I rarely pay attention to people's non-verbal cues (such as body language or facial expressions)

5. I prepare what I'm going to say in response while the other person is still talking
6. If I disagree with people, I interrupt them immediately to set the record straight
7. If the other person is long winded or boring, I stop listening
8. When I know what people are going to say, I don't wait for them to finish but answer right away
9. When I stop paying attention to someone I try to look like I'm listening anyway
10. I often interrupt people to speed along a conversation

So, how did you do? Obviously in this test, the more 'negative responses you have the better listener you are. For most people, getting half of these as 'No' would be a great result. Listening is a skill. It's an area we need to practice to get better like most other skills.

Think about this yourself and what you find yourself doing in conversations. In coaching it should be no different. You want to avoid being automatically ready with your response when the person has finished speaking. You need to be interested in them and their responses. Avoid saying, "Yes" to them and immediately head off in another direction. If you agree with someone (or not) add a relevant comment about that point before moving on. It shows you were listening properly and have taken it in. Then you can change direction or the conversation easily. In a lot of cases, people aren't really listening to each other; they are just taking turns to speak.

Listening doesn't mean not talking. In fact, the best listeners are talking too. They are almost facilitating the conversation, asking clarifying questions (see questioning next), checking for understanding, responding with empathetic statements such as, "Wow, that must have really been a struggle for you" and at the very least nodding or giving non-verbal cues that they are engaged, comprehending and involved in the discussion that's occurring.

Reflective listening is when we are using questions to clarify our understanding or showing that we understand by using supportive statements.

Active listening is the use of non-verbal responses such as nodding, eye contact or facial expressions or even encouraging verbal indicators such as "Uh huh, yes, wow etc."

In all of these areas of listening, pausing before your response should be a consideration. If we don't pause, we really aren't giving our brains an opportunity to let the other person's words sink in.

## Questioning skills

Knowing how to ask the right questions can save time, create the right atmosphere and avoid slipping into a 'telling' mode. When people think about different types of questions, the standard responses are 'Open' and 'Closed'. Well, they are the two most basic types of questions, sure but there are others that can have an impact which are varieties of both the standard open and closed question types.

Let's look at the two basic questions first anyway:

**OPEN** questions start with:

- How
- Why
- Where
- What
- When
- Who

That's it. There aren't any other ways to start an open question. Why is it called an open question? Well, starting a question with one of these words is more likely to engage the other person to provide an answer that requires more than just a one word response. There's actually no real guarantee to that, but the chances are much higher.

For example: "How do you think the session is going?" should open up the opportunity for the respondent to share their thoughts on the session. Of course, they could just say "Fine". That's when you would follow up with another open question such as, "What exactly do you think is fine about it?" which will give them more of a reason to share their thoughts.

**CLOSED** questions have a lot more ways of starting. Some examples include:

- Should
- Did
- Can
- Will
- Could
- Shall

Closed questions normally provide the respondent with the option of a one word response which is often 'Yes' or 'No'.

For example: "Can you write this down?" will mean the other person is going to either say 'Yes' or 'No'.

Knowing this basic information can help us in our coaching. If we want the person to share their thoughts and feelings on something – the obvious way to get them to talk or 'open up' is to ask an 'Open' question. If we want to clarify something, then a 'Closed' question will do it.

Then there are a number of other question types that can be applied to these Open or Closed questions. These include:

**Leading Question** – this is where you would ask a question towards a type of response you want to hear. For example, "What did you like about the presentation?" is effectively leading the other person to tell you what they liked about it. There isn't much room for another response unless they liked nothing about it at all. Of course you can have an open leading or a closed leading question.

**Echoic Question** – this is where you repeat back part of a statement to the person that just said something to you. This is especially useful if you didn't hear a part of their sentence or want to clarify a component of what they said. For example, if someone was giving you their address and you didn't hear the name of the street correctly, as in "I live at 245 'urrrmm' Street", you would respond by asking, "You live at 245 'what' street?" This tells the other person that you heard everything else okay – it was just the street name they need to repeat a bit more clearly.

**Rhetorical Question** – these are questions that don't require a response. They often don't sound like actual questions. For example, "I wonder what would happen if we all got sick at once?" Sometimes a rhetorical question is used just to get people to think about something rather than come up with an immediate solution or response.

**Clarifying Question** – Use these to check your understanding or to delve a bit deeper into a part of the discussion. These types of questions can be structured like, "Are you saying that they didn't care about what they did?" This will give the other person an opportunity to either confirm what you asked or clarify something different.

**Direct Question** – we don't often use direct questions. We tend to soften them up a bit. For example, the direct question, "Where's the bus station?" is often asked after a softener statement like, "Excuse me, I'm a little lost. Where's the bus station?"

Of course, you could actually ask a question in another way. For example, if you are struggling to get someone to open up and talk to you, try the phrase, "Tell me about..." This is not a question as such but acts like a question in getting them to talk to you. Try it out next time you need some help in getting someone to talk to you. I find this especially useful for my children. When I ask, "What did you do today?" They often respond with shrugged shoulders or the one word answer, "Stuff." Yet, when I change it to; "Tell me about your day." I get a little more information.

## Paraphrasing

In order for us to ensure that we have understood someone correctly or for us to know whether someone has understood us correctly, we can use the communication tool known as paraphrasing. This is basically defined as saying something back to someone in our own words. It is not repeating verbatim. That only shows that we can copy what the other person has said. When we say it back in our own words, we have to internalise it and translate it into a way we may have said it.

Think about someone who has to communicate in a language foreign to their native language. They have to follow four steps:

1. They hear what is said in the foreign language

2. They translate what was said into their native language

3. They formulate their response in their native language

4. They translate their response into the foreign language

That's quite a task. It can be exhausting and it takes time. However, it helps to internalise what is said. This is the same as paraphrasing. We internalise what is said, translate it into our words and say it back again.

When we paraphrase, we give the other person a chance to confirm what we heard was what the other person meant to say. It's a simple act but it can save so much trouble. Taking an extra few seconds to ensure we have it right or that the person we are talking with has understood what we say can save time, errors and extra effort.

As far as communication goes, it's a tool that should be used much more often.

## Tone of voice

All too often we focus on the words that we use rather than the way we use them. It's true that words are important. In the field of Law, if you don't read the 'fine print' (the words), then you could get into trouble. However, as you'll see in the 'Body Language' paragraphs following, the words only account for a small part of the impact of what is being said.

Let's take for example the phrase:

"Who did this?"

Now depending on how this is said, the reaction of those around will be quite different. If the phrase was said in a delighted tone, it's likely to bring everyone forward seeking to take the credit.

However, if the same phrase was said in an angry tone, you are likely to get the opposite response. If you're uncertain as to how this works, try it out at home. My kids tend to all rush in when the 'delighted' tone is used and hide when the 'angry' tone is employed.

There are many tones we can add too. Tones are ways of speaking and the list is pretty huge. Some examples include:

- Angry
- Happy
- Bored
- Amorous
- Embarrassed
- Sad
- Condescending

- Frustrated
- Amazed
- Confused
- Excited
- Friendly
- Anxious
- Scared

Why don't you practice saying a shopping list in different tones to someone and see if they can guess which tone you're using. They'll usually be right.

In a coaching situation, you can also change the whole meaning of a sentence by where you put the biggest emphasis. The intonation of the voice can alter meaning dramatically.

Take this sentence for example:

"I never said you could leave early"

It seems pretty harmless right?

Okay – let's look at changing the intonation (the emphasis) of each word in turn and look at what it does to the sentence:

| **Phrase** | **Means** |
| --- | --- |
| "**I** never said you could leave early" – | someone may have said you could leave early but it wasn't me. |
| "I **never** said you could leave early" - | I deny ever saying that you could leave early. |
| "I never **said** you could leave early" - | I may have implied that you could leave early but didn't actually say it. |
| "I never said **you** could leave early" - | Someone else may be leaving early but not you. |
| "I never said you **could** leave early" - | We may have talked about leaving early but I never confirmed it. |
| "I never said you could **leave** early" - | There may be something you could do early but it wasn't "leaving". |
| "I never said you could leave **early**" - | You can leave alright but not early. |

So, as you can see, the placement of the emphasis can alter the meaning of a simple seven word sentence a lot. Why is this important? Well it's not just about the way YOU say something – as in when you are speaking with someone – that's very important. It's also about how the other person takes what is said. So if you speak with a monotone voice (no change in pitch or variance) then emphasis can seemingly be nowhere and if you decide to write the feedback down – or send it by email, you open yourself up to the other person's interpretation. That can depend on their current state of mind, their setting, their last interaction with you – a whole host of different impacts. If you can read a simple seven word sentence seven different ways – imagine how many ways you could take a lengthy email on how your performance was going!

If you're going to give feedback – give it verbally. Use email only as confirmation. Feedback should always be a verbal process. It's the only way an exchange of understanding can take place.

## *Body language*

When we communicate in a face to face setting, body language contributes the most to our communication. It's more than the tone of voice we use and the actual words we speak. In fact, the words we speak have the least value of all three components. In studies conducted in the 1960s by Albert Mehrabian, the statistics showed that 7% were attributed to Words, 38% to tone of voice and 55% to non-verbal cues – such as body language or facial expression. In non-face-to-face communication such as telephone communication, these figures change to 85% tone of voice and 7% words. *

There is no doubt that the words are important but you can see how much the tone of voice can change the way those words can be taken. Adding to that, the way we look, stand, hold our arms, frown, smile, stomp up and down, play with our hair – everything physically will also add an angle on our wording.

In coaching, the use of all three components should be uniform; our words, our tone and our body language should all be contributing to the same message.

* - *Mehrabian's studies actually referred to communication about feelings and attitudes. Although these statistics have been generally accepted for all communication, Mehrabian states on his website that they are only confirmed for the subject of his experiments. See www.kaaj.com/psych*

## *Parent / child language*

An area that is commonly utilised to ill effect is the parent/child languages between a leader and a team member. This is manifested in one of two ways normally. Firstly, the leader takes the role of the critical parent and their language takes the form of scolding or of a critical nature. Questions like:

"Why did you do this?" and "How did you let this happen?"

These focus on judging the behaviour of the team member and not focusing on the situation.

Similarly, the opposite approach is the nurturing parent who uses phrases like:

"That's okay. You're doing fine." And "Don't worry; I'll sort that out for you."

In both extremes, there's either a lecture or a rescue coming and neither really helps the team member to grow or develop. In communicating with the team, consider a more facilitated approach along the lines of questioning like:

"Is there another way you could say that?" and "Can you tell me how you came to that decision?"

Remember that as the leader, you are there to help develop your teams. Give them opportunities to think and to develop accountability, empowerment and decision making skills.

> **Tip:** Although it's basic, learn to communicate so that there is always an exchange of understanding. Don't assume you have communicated.

# Effective coaching & feedback

To coach someone is different than mentoring someone. Mentoring is about showing a person how to do or become something. It encompasses sharing what the mentor has done to be successful or how to accomplish a task. There's more telling and showing than there is in coaching.

Coaching is about carrying, transporting or moving somebody from one state or place to another. It is really about helping people resolve their own issues and discover their own potential. Coaching is not about lecturing or telling people what to do or solving all their problems. Although you may need to instruct or direct from time to time, the major role of a coach is to help the person being coached to find the solution themselves. This method of self-discovery is a fundamental leadership skill and can make all the difference.

If you believe you are coaching someone else because you are more capable than the other person, you are looking at coaching incorrectly. In many cases, the person being coached will know more about the systems, processes, products, services and even customers than you will. It's not about being the hero or the rescuer. It's not about looking smart or showing that you know everything. It's about helping people know how to come to solutions on their own, developing strategies for a better way of thinking and facilitating issues so they have total ownership.

You can do all this by developing your own questioning, listening and paraphrasing skills. As a coach, you need to develop skills in 'drawing' information out of people.

The aim of good coaching is to facilitate a discussion. This means that your task is to 'draw out' information from the person you are coaching. It's about helping them to discover the answers and solutions for themselves. Self-discovery is a term to be aware of as a leader. Use it to ensure you are not just lecturing or telling people what to do.

## *Reinforcing feedback*

There are two basic types of coaching or giving feedback.

The first is Reinforcing or encouraging feedback. This is when you are feeding back to the individual that what they have done or are doing is the right thing. It helps if this is done as soon as possible after the behaviour is demonstrated. This is when the impact is greatest. The Time / Impact curve demonstrates this:

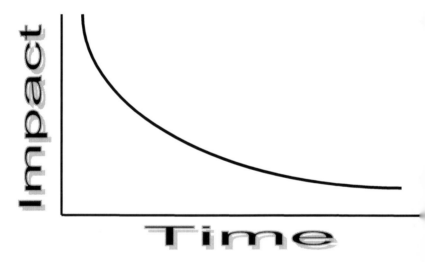

The longer you leave something, the less the impact has on the individual.

This type of feedback helps to show people that they are on the right track and is especially helpful if the behaviour (what they did or said) was linked to the outcome or result. A person will gain so much more from a conversation that doesn't just centre on WHAT they did but WHY they did it. Linking the WHY to the result will help reinforce the reasons for continuing (or stopping) a certain behaviour. Coaching is not cheerleading and leaders, managers and coaches must recognise the difference. Just saying 'you did a great job there' or 'that was nice work' will not reinforce strongly enough the behaviour you want them to continue using. It needs to be followed by a discussion on why is was a great job or why it was excellent and what the impact was on the outcome because of what they did or said.

In reinforcing feedback, you would describe what has been done and discuss the impact it has had. For example, if a staff member had resolved a query and then explained to the customer that to save time on their next query they could register it on the website and someone would call them back at a convenient time for them, the leader could coach on that the following way:

> "When you offered that service to the customer about registering future queries that way, you really added some great value that they weren't expecting. It shows you understand the future needs of the customer extremely well. You didn't have to say it, but you did and that customer has a better view of our company as a result. Great work. Keep it up."

The staff member would feel acknowledged, reassured for giving the information and great about what they did as well as having the reasons reinforced by their leader. Everyone wins.

## Corrective feedback

The other type of feedback is corrective feedback or developmental feedback and focuses on what they can improve on. This can also be done in a positive manner and is often avoided in 'poor coaching' because coaches don't want to 'hurt feelings' or engage in conflict, or are just not sure how to do it.

This is best done just before the person has an opportunity to use it. This means that it is often wasted at the end of the day for example as they will just be reflecting on the feedback and not on the impact it could have.

This type of feedback is well done if you are coaching someone live in a setting where you are taking calls together, making sales visits or in the work environment live. For example, if you wanted a staff member to try out a new technique to pause after asking for a sale, you could say,

> "Okay, on this next call, after you have asked them for the business, just pause and don't say anything until they speak next. Let them speak first okay?"

Once the staff member tries it out and sees the effect, they'll have additional confidence in what you've told them and keep using it. If you said it a week earlier, there's little chance they will remember to do it and therefore not reap any associated benefits.

In giving corrective feedback, it is important to help the person being coached see things as facts rather than your opinion. Facts always mean that there is something concrete and less to argue over.

Remember, for feedback to be valuable, it needs to be done right! If I say "you are a great worker" or "you're fantastic" it is general and non-specific and does not mean much. Or if I say "You look sloppy today" or "You are not a good worker", you could feel upset and get defensive.

If we give non-specific feedback we'll often get a defensive response, like "what do you mean?"

All feedback then should be descriptive rather than evaluative. Descriptive feedback focuses on stating the facts while evaluative feedback focuses on your opinion.

Here are some examples:

**Behaviour:** Person comes to work without a name badge on:

**Evaluative Feedback:** "You're sloppy"

**Descriptive Feedback:** "You don't have your name badge on"

**Behaviour:** Person comes into work ten minutes late:

**Evaluative Feedback:** "You don't care about your work very much"

**Descriptive Feedback:** "I see you are late this morning"

**Behaviour:** Person shouts across the office

**Evaluative Feedback:** "You got really angry back then"

**Descriptive Feedback**: "You raised your voice in that conversation"

You can see that the descriptive feedback can then lead you into a proper discussion about the behaviour exerted. Evaluative feedback could lead the other person to disagree with you and argue another reason for the behaviour.

**Positive and negative feedback**

There's no getting away from it, people will still view receiving feedback as either positive or negative feedback. We have dressed it up in different words here but in the end someone will feel like they are being praised or criticised. It's important to recognise what impact each has on the performance of the individual and ultimately the wider teams. The University of Michigan Business School did a study in which they compared team performance to the frequency of praise and criticism given within teams. The best performing teams used about six times as many positive comments in feedback for every negative one.

In your feedback, remember that to make a positive impact on your teams, you really need to remember that figure. Six to one is quite a high ratio but can make the difference from a low to average performance grow to a high performance.

## Coaching the right way

In order to coach the right way, we need to understand what the wrong way is. Let's face it, we have all had some experience where coaching hasn't been very effective. In fact, I have had organisations say to me that they have regular coaching but nothing changes. Their leaders coach each month, people commit and then hold the same conversations the next month again with no change. This is a classic example of coaching on activators in order to change behaviours.

Activators are those items that cause us to do something. In themselves they have some motivation behind them. For example, an activator we all have is hunger. This activator leads us to do a certain behaviour which is to feed ourselves. This behaviour leads to a consequence which is that we become full (or put on weight)! So, there are three components in this process:

The activator is the driver of the behaviour.

The behaviour is what is done.

The consequence is the result.

Coaching that is not done well is coaching that is focused on the activator. This is coaching that focuses on words like, "do more, do better, faster, increase, slow down, improve" etc. People then under pressure or wishing to please say, "Okay". Leaders then feel they have a commitment and are surprised that the behaviour hasn't changed. They then coach more and say the same stuff but louder, bolder etc.

However, if the consequence is changed, the behaviour is much more likely to be altered. Think about these two examples:

1. If you were thirsty (activator) and you put $2 in a drinks machine (behaviour) you would expect a drink (consequence). However, if the drink did not come out as a result, you are not likely to keep putting $2 in the machine. The consequence is dramatically different that it has changed your behaviour. You are more likely to kick the machine or call someone up about it rather than keep putting money in.
2. If the room got dark as a result of the sun going down (activator) and you turned the light switch on (behaviour) you would expect the light to come on (consequence). However, if the light did not work, you would not keep turning the light switch on (apart from that frantic on/off pressing until you realised it won't work). You would source an alternative light source like a torch.

So, you can see that with these two examples, the change in the consequence made a huge impact on the actual behaviour exhibited.

Now think about your people and their roles. What example can you start with where you want behaviour to change? What is the activator and the normal consequence? What can you change the consequence to be in order for the behaviour to change?

Some coaching is done to tick a box. I.e. a leader feels they must coach so they do (not very well) and tick the coaching box. Coaching is not a passive action; it needs to be engaging, thought through and personal to the individual. You cannot hope to coach everybody the same way. People in your team will have preferences and needs that vary.

**Tip:** Focus on changing the consequence to successfully change the behaviour.

# The brain and coaching

When the brain is exposed to a new stimulus of any type – image, smell, voice, sensation etc, there is a lot of activity. Neurons are firing all over the brain as it searches for some recognition or place of reference for the stimulus. Eventually, it will store the stimulus somewhere for accessing again. The second time the brain encounters the same stimulus, there is still a lot of brain activity but not as much as the first time. The brain locates the initial stored stimulus and recognises the original stimulus. Third and subsequent times, the brain more quickly accesses the stored information and eventually, the stimulus creates a 'hard wired' reaction where the brain doesn't have to run through much accessing but knows where to find the response that's generally required for that stimulus.

Those hard wired reactions are what we call habitual. They are automatic pilot responses and ways of dealing with things. Each of us develops these 'hard wired' reactions over time for lots of things. At work, we become quite proficient in what we do because we have 'hard wired' the processes. Very often, we don't have to think too hard about all that we do – it's automatic. Our staff too have this 'hard wiring' going on when they do things such as talking to customers, habits for the way they talk to customers, methods they use to shortcut the systems they use, responses they rely on to deal with situations etc.

Some of those habits however aren't what we want to see or are not the way they should be approaching their work. Our job then is to break that hard wiring and help them to find new routes in the brain. This can be quite hard. Think of a habit you have that you have tried to break. It's not that easy, is it? Unless you have a better alternative or some driving desire, you probably won't change. However, sometimes you do change. Why is that? Well, think about it this way. You probably have a favourite restaurant or holiday spot. That only became your favourite after someone introduced it to you or you were exposed to it. Before then, some other place was your favourite. For us then in coaching, we need to expose our coachees to other alternatives; ideas that can lead them to substitute their current habit for a new one. One that will improve their performance, reaction from customers or whatever it is we are coaching them on.

Just like the example of motivation, we don't do that by externally imposing something. We know that doesn't work. We need to create an internal motivation to change.

So, tapping in to a person's motivation is the sure way to get them to improve performance, correct mistakes and sustain the change. There are ten basic principles for coaching and feedback success that we'll now discuss.

## *Why coach?*

Coaching is really about helping people resolve their own issues and discover their own potential. Coaching is not about lecturing or telling people what to do or solving all their problems. Although you may need to instruct or direct from time to time, the major role of a coach is to help the coachee find the solution themselves. So, what are the purposes of coaching? Well, there are many reasons to coach – here's a few:

**Development:**       Develop further understanding or skills of others

**Facilitate:**       Help others discover new ways of doing things, resolve issues and identify fixes

**Training:**       Up skill in new areas and techniques

**Correct mistakes:**       Help identify errors and change those behaviours

**Give praise:**       Encourage others and congratulate them on good work, consistent good behaviour, results that have exceeded expectation etc

**Delegate:**       Help develop others through delegation

**Regulate:**       Achieve consistency through standards followed up by coaching

—— ——

# The 10 key principles of effective coaching

Although there are many principles of quality coaching techniques, there are some that will have the biggest impact on those being coached and the effectiveness of the experience for both parties. Organisations may coach regularly and have good systems in place to ensure a positive coaching culture is in place. However, for some people, nothing seems to change. People are coached on a regular basis but no behavioural change takes place. This is normally down to the fact that the coaching is ineffective. The physical act of coaching is taking place but the mental shift, desire or drive has not been engaged.

Consider the following ten principles as those that have been identified as those that can help you as a coach have maximum impact for your coaching success. Consider that we are all on a quest to continuously learn and adapt, so don't stop your research in to ways and techniques that can improve your style, strengthen your approach and increase your abilities as a coach.

# Principle 1: Coach the individual

The first basic for coaching is to realise that each person is different and they will require some individual attention and approach in regards to feedback and coaching. Some people will be very sensitive and embarrassed to be given constructive feedback and may need some confidence boosting first while others will want to dispense with any pleasantries and get straight into areas of improvement. You can't treat these two extremes the same.

There isn't just one model of feedback and one way of coaching that works but there are plenty that don't.

In order to know how to approach each person, you need to know a bit about them. What type of learning style do they have? What is their personality type? What do they like to do in their spare time? Who do they hang around with at work? What are some of the strengths you have noticed about them? What makes them smile? Why do they work where they do? These are just a few of the questions that knowing the answer to will help you in your role as a coach.

If you know their best learning style (audio, visual or kinaesthetic), you will know how best to approach your coaching with them. For audio preferences you can ensure that you engage in good discussion, play back a recorded call to them if possible, get them to listen to a good and bad example of a conversation etc. For visual learners, write things down, show them graphs, trends or diagrams and keep plenty of colour going. Show them things on the computer screen and describe things by way of the 'big picture' – how does what they do impact on the rest of the organisation or the customer. For kinaesthetic preferences, ensure that they are involved doing something. Don't just show them – let them do it. Practice doing role plays and have them offer suggestions. These people learn best by doing.

So how do you know which preference your people have? You can run a simple AVK test (there are loads of free ones on the internet). You can listen to the way they talk – do they use audio language (I hear what you're saying, that sounds great etc) or visual language (I see what you mean, I can see where this is going, I can picture that etc) or Kinaesthetic language (I feel for you, it just doesn't feel right etc). Or you can just simply ask them what they prefer – it can be that simple!

Personality styles can also provide you with clues as to how people like to be coached and receive feedback. Some people like recognition – so you can get them to accept challenges with a promise of such. Some people want to avoid conflict, so approach the situation by putting them at ease etc.

In short, you need to come off the 'auto pilot' and be in a conscious state when coaching. You can't assume that everyone is happy with your standard default approach and remember that each individual is just that – an individual who needs their kind of attention. The golden rule states that you should treat people as you wish to be treated. Well that's not going to work in coaching and feedback sessions. You need to live the platinum rule which is to treat people as <u>they</u> wish to be treated.

---

**Tip:** Get to know the person you are coaching. Ask them their preferences. If they're not sure, give them some options.

---

# Principle 2: Know several ways to coach

As a coach and knowing the key point about coaching others as individuals, means that you then need to have several tools in your toolkit of ways to effectively coach and give feedback. It's impossible to coach everyone the way they need to be coached with one dimensional coaching abilities. It's your role to look for, learn and master several coaching skills and feedback techniques.

There isn't one right way to coach and the more techniques you learn, the better equipped you'll be to coach more diverse people. The key though is not knowing more ways to coach on its own, it's knowing which ones to use and when.

In this chapter, we will look at a couple of feedback models. You can also look at the chapter dealing with formal and informal coaching for more ideas on this.

Feedback models are important as they give some structure around giving feedback. Here we will look at two models (4 steps process and DESCCO).

## 4 steps process: Ask, Tell, Ask, Tell

Step 1: In this process, as the coach you direct the conversation by first asking them a question such as: "What do you think went well in that sales call?" You then listen to the individual share their thoughts on the matter.

Step 2: Next, you tell them what you think went well in that sales call. It may be that you confirm what they have said and elaborate a little more. People like to hear specifics about things. Think about the time you may have spoken at an event, written a report or performed on stage. If someone comes up to you and says, "Great job – I really enjoyed what you did!" Well, you feel good about it – but how much better and more sincere does it sound when someone adds something like, "I especially liked it when you did xxx". Adding that little bit of extra information helps you feel that they took something in, that it meant something to them and that they were attentive.

Step 3: You follow up your comments by asking another question based around what they think they would do differently next time. As an example, "what would you do differently if you could do it over?" or "what do you think you could improve on next time?" these questions are not negatively geared. The first example especially only asks for 'different' not 'better'. When people feel like the pressure is off a bit and don't have to come up with something better, just different, it's much easier.

Step 4: Finally, you tell them what they could do differently. Again, you may confirm what they have said, or you may elaborate further.

This simple four steps process is a model that can be used to engage people in conversation and gets them thinking about what they have done and ways to look at it differently.

In summary, the Four Step Process is:

**Step One:**    **Ask them what went well**

**Step Two:**    **Tell them what you thought went well**

**Step Three:**  **Ask them what they could have done differently**

**Step Four:**   **Tell them what you think they could have done differently**

To enhance this experience further, you may also like to add some other questions at each step. Ensure that the questions have some meaning and make a point and also add value. For example, after any of the responses, you could ask something like, "And what impact might that have had on the customer?" Getting them to think about the consequence of the responded action will help further embed reasoning into what they or you have said.

Here's how the whole conversation could go. Let's take a phone coaching situation where the coach is listening in on a double headset. It could just as easily be a situation where a sales manager has joined one of their sales team on a series of sales calls face to face with customers.

**Coach:** "Okay John, what do you think you did well on that call?"

**Customer Rep:** "Well, I certainly solved the query she had and I think she went away happy. I also feel like I spoke clearly so she could understand"

**Coach:** "Yes, I think she certainly got the answer she needed and won't need to call back for anything and I like the way you got her to paraphrase back your answer to make sure she understood. Great. Now what could you have done differently?"

**Customer Rep:** "Ummm, I'm not sure."

**Coach:** "Thinking about the way you addressed the person, is there anything you could have changed?"

**Customer Rep:** "Oh, do you mean about the way I used 'Madam'?"

**Coach:** "Yes, that's right. At the start of the call, she called herself Mrs Garcia twice which indicated that her preference for addressing her is that way. How do you think using the customer's name like that might have changed the way the call went?"

| | |
|---|---|
| **Customer Rep:** | "Well, I suppose it would have made it more personal." |
| **Coach:** | "That's right, it would. When you call companies, do you like to be treated personally?" |
| **Customer Rep:** | "Well, yes, I suppose I do." |
| **Coach:** | "Ok then. Let's look at that on the next call. I think that will make quite a difference from the customer perspective." |

There are so many ways to conduct this type of feedback model. You may like to change it around a bit to: ASK, ASK, TELL, TELL. You may even want to just ASK. The important thing is to get the individual to talk, keep it specific and help them during the conversation to get to the points you want them to make where necessary.

## DESCCO

The second feedback model to explain to you is the DESCCO method. Here, we have an acronym for the words:

**D**escribe the behaviour

**E**xpress how you felt

**S**pecify what you'd prefer

**C**onsequences of the new action

**C**ontract to act in the new way

**O**k

Like the Ask Tell process above, there are many ways to use the DESCCO model. Firstly, if you wanted to give direct feedback to someone say for shouting across a room, you might use it like this:

"John, when you shouted across the office, I felt like you distracted everyone else from their work. If you want my attention, I'd prefer it if you walked over to my office and spoke with me. That way, you won't be disturbing everybody else and potentially distracting them in their work flow. So, can I expect you to not shout next time you want me for something? Okay."

So, you'll see in that short paragraph that we used all the steps of DESCCO in a simple flow:

**Describe**: "When you shouted across the office..."

**Express**: "I felt like you distracted everyone else from their work."

**Specify**: "I'd prefer it if you walked over to my office..."

**Consequences**: "That way, you won't be disturbing everybody..."

**Contract**: "So, can I expect you to not shout..."

**Ok**: "Okay."

Each of the steps has an important element to play in helping people to alter their behaviour. Firstly, describing what they did helps the person know exactly what it is you're talking about. It's therefore much more useful if the feedback given is descriptive (i.e. factual). The expression component then personalises it and gives some meaning to the effect of their behaviour. Specifying another way of approaching it gives them an alternative and explaining the consequences (which could be good or bad) gives reasoning for the person to consider the new behaviour suggestion. The contract is a way of getting them to concur or show their understanding. The ending with 'Okay' is for them to agree.

In our example above, we have shown a direct 'telling' method of giving feedback. Of course, it can be even more powerful if you switch the 'telling' to 'asking' in each of the steps of the DESCCO process after the 'Describe' step. For example, "When you shouted across the office, what impact do you think that had on the rest of the team?" This way you will be able to uncover their understanding and thinking a lot sooner and potentially gain greater buy-in. This method is discussed in greater depth in Principle 4: 'Encourage Self Discovery'.

There are many models for giving feedback. Some people won't want you to go through a process like the four steps – they may prefer just to be told what they need to do to improve. It's therefore very important that Principle 1: 'Coach the individual' is adhered to in the first instance and find out how they best respond to coaching.

> **Tip:** Learn a few coaching and feedback models like Ask Tell and DESCCO. Practice them at home on family or with friends. Do some role plays with someone you are comfortable with.

## Principle 3: Don't just tick boxes

Several people have said to me in the past, "Well, we do coaching regularly but nothing changes." Going back to the section on motivation, most people see the need for coaching, so they do it but for a lot of people, the coach isn't converted. The coach doesn't have buy-in and at best 'accepts' that it needs to be done. The problem isn't with the coachee – it's with the coach! These might be harsh words – but they are true (in most cases).

One of the big traps to fall into is to get into a routine of doing something because it should be done. In a lot of cases, it might as well never be done for all the benefit that comes. Coaching is not a register. It's not a checklist. It's also not a lecture. If our approach is all about making sure we coach a certain number of times and cover off the minimum number of points, we have done just that – we might have achieved our goal (coaching each team member every two weeks say) but our objective to help people improve performance has been missed by a mile.

So, when coaching, we need to have a purpose. Ask yourself the question, "What is it I really want to see as a result of this coaching session?" or "What will tell me this session has been worthwhile?" or even "What do I want to see next for this person?" Have a purpose, have a reason for the coaching session to go ahead. This might need some planning time. Be prepared. The coachee deserves a bit of preparation. Sure, they need to be engaged too – but the onus is on you as the coach to run the session and direct the result.

Look to make the change in the individual. Rather than closing the session wondering if anything will be different from then on – have the goal that something *will* be different by the end of the session. Of course, this means you need to have some focus on what would be reasonable, what needs to change, how can you help the individual see the benefits of changing and how will you know that they are on board with it all. Well a lot of that will depend on your preparation or observation skills and on how you run the session.

Think about the times you have had a change of mind or found something new and from then on run with it. What about a restaurant that you love or a meal that's become your favourite? Perhaps it is a new item of clothing, a movie, a book or a holiday destination. All of these things would once have been introduced to you at some point. Now before that time, something else was your favourite meal, your favourite movie etc. Now, however, it's all different because you have changed you preference. You have had a new experience; you've seen something different in it that makes you prefer to do, say, eat or experience that over other options. That's the sort of experience we should look to create with our coachees.

Rather than just ticking boxes, work at having effective conversations. What will make a change in this individual? How can I get them to really think about consequences (good or bad) for doing something? What impact will their behaviour have on the customer, their job or their colleagues? The sorts of questions we can look at in the following section will be ideal places to start where we look at how to Encourage Self Discovery.

> **Tip:** Before you begin coaching, consider what you really want this person to get out of the session. If you're not sure before you start, take time before you conclude to sum up and get a firm action from them.

## Principle 4: Encourage self-discovery

There are varying schools of thought on what ratio the coaching discussion should go in regards to the amount of talking from each party. It wouldn't be too far off the mark though to suggest 70:30 in favour of the coachee, where the coach effectively facilitates the discussion to draw out information and suggestions from the coachee.

Sometimes as coaches, we feel that we have the knowledge and the fastest and best way to share it is to tell, tell, tell. Consider the effectiveness of that ideology. The old adage goes:

**If you tell me, I'll probably forget**
**If you show me I might remember**
**If you involve me, I'll understand**

When we get involved, we not only stand a better chance of remembering something, we also get to understand why and how it all works. Think about a time you needed directions to drive somewhere. If you were told directions, you may have struggled your way there and even got a little lost on the way. If you were a passenger, you have a better chance of remembering the route BUT if you drove there yourself, you will more likely remember the route best.

Learning a new skill takes involvement. You can read all you like about how to swim – but until you get into the water – you won't actually learn.

So, the ability to get the other person to try and figure out an answer or solution will help them immensely over just telling them. We all benefit more when we have had to struggle a bit. The result is more valuable to us. We had to earn it. By the same token though, don't leave them floundering. If they need a nudge – help them in the right direction.

We looked at the DESCCO method earlier on. Rather than using the direct tell, tell, tell approach we first looked at, how about asking the individual the questions? Flip it round a bit. For example, let's say you wanted to address the issue that they had shouted across the office to get someone's attention. You could start by addressing the behaviour thus, "When you shouted across the office...how do you think it made everybody else feel?" This covers off the 'Describe' and 'Express' components of DESCCO. But, rather than you telling them how it made you or others feel – you have asked them to put themselves in other's shoes.

Then go to the next step and 'specify' by asking "What would have been another way to handle that?" Let them answer and encourage them where needed. Then follow up with the 'consequences' "And what might be the result of that?" You are likely to get a response that will just need a confirmation from you and you can finish off with "Exactly, so next time you need to get hold of someone quickly, will you do it that way?" Ok.

You don't have to use the DESCCO method – that's just an example but get them to think. You don't have to show them you know everything by telling them – you can show them by asking them and confirming if you like – that way you don't sound like your force feeding them but helping them see that they know the answers already themselves.

If they just aren't getting it and need some help, be more specific. Let's say you were coaching someone on a conversation they had and you asked them how they could improve and they couldn't think of anything, ask a follow up question about the specific area of the conversation. If the ending was bad – ask them how they could improve the ending.

The best way to get buy-in from someone else is to help them come up with the idea or at least help them think it was their idea. Draw out of the individual what they think is acceptable or right or the best way to handle something. This method of coaching or working with people is known as facilitation. It can be defined as the act of assisting or making easier the progress or improvement of something. Normally, facilitation would be used in the context of a group where the facilitator would be there to help the group to have an effective dialog without taking any side of the argument, especially in order to reach a consensus. In a one-on-one situation, the facilitator, or coach, can also be there to help guide the discussion effectively to a certain destination.

In essence, the self-discovery component focuses on helping the individual being coached to come up with a reasonable response or suggestion that they can own. They may need some guidance but you should avoid giving them the answers or jumping straight into the 'telling' mode unless absolutely necessary.

**Tip:**   Getting the other person to talk is the key. Ask questions and avoid 'telling'. When you feel like you're about to give the solution, ask a question about it first.

## Principle 5: Look for the cause

Most of us will have been to the doctor in order to be diagnosed for a cure to be given for a number of symptoms we have. You will have noticed on a trip to the doctors or hospital that you will have been asked a number of questions. These questions are designed to help determine the cause of the symptoms that you have. Let's say you have constant headaches. There could be lots of causes for those headaches but if the doctor merely prescribed a headache tablet for example, it may not cure you of the headaches ongoing. The doctor's job is to identify what is causing the headaches and treat that cause – not just the symptom.

The popular TV series in the late 2000's called 'House' is an ideal example of how the doctors have to find the actual cause of the symptoms displayed. If they don't identify the root cause, the treating of the symptoms would be often fruitless and pointless.

In your role as a coach, one of the key aspects is to try to uncover the reasons why somebody may not be doing what they should. The skills of using self-discovery could be very useful here.

Let's take an example here of someone not using your knowledge base to look up information for a customer when it is obvious to you that it may help give valuable information. To you, that may be just fundamental in order to service the customer. You may be tempted to just tell the person to start using it. After all, it's there and it's useful. If, however, the person is a little phobic when it comes to computers, they may not want to use it. Maybe they haven't had enough training on it. Perhaps they have used it in the past and it didn't really help them. They may have tried using it and find it very slow and therefore a hindrance when talking to the customer. Any one of these or perhaps other reasons could exist and each one will require a different tact in dealing with the issue – as follows:

| Reason | Action |
| --- | --- |
| Don't like computers | Give them some training |
| Didn't help in the past | Review the example and share personal experience. Look for something that's helped you |
| System too slow | Jump on the system with them and see for yourself – get them to show you. Report to IT |
| Not sure how to use it | Show them. Give them some scheduled training |

Treating the cause will alleviate the issues faced with frustration because you feel like you keep telling someone but they don't change.

As an opportunity to practice this, ask the individual the two main reasons they can see why they don't do something. If they struggle to come up with an answer – give them a couple of options. Then ask the important question, "If we could fix that, would you do it?" – (or the equivalent relevant question).

**Tip:** Avoid the temptation to act on the first response. Dig a little deeper for the root cause.

## Principle 6: Be present and focus

One of the four main principles of the FISH! Philosophy established by John Christensen is 'Be There' or 'Be Present' which has more to do with giving your full attention to a task or individual. We expect our staff members to focus on their tasks - especially when they are engaged with customers, so it's right that we are focusing on the individuals in coaching. We may feel that we can multitask, but let's face it; some multi-tasking is just like being all over the place.

In order for us to fully comprehend our staff and to catch all the nuances and potential reasons behind their statements etc., we need to give them our full attention. At the very least, it's common courtesy to be fully engaged in a coaching session anyway. If we aren't prepared to listen intently or if we allow ourselves to drift into 'auto pilot' because we've 'heard this all before' or we 'think' we know where this is going, then we may miss something vital.

There are some famous words penned by the Georgian poet, William Henry Davies, "No matter where this body is, the mind is free to go elsewhere." We can be physically present but mentally far away from what we're actually doing. We've all experienced trying to get someone's attention and not got it completely or we've been in a conversation and noticed a pause when we weren't really paying attention and then had the awful feeling of knowing that we were just asked a question and never heard it. It's a little embarrassing and it certainly isn't professional.

Even if we are having the coaching session but we're trying to finish something off first, it's not giving the other person the right signals to make them wait as we are effectively saying that something else is more important than them.

If we want our teams to get switched on to coaching and look forward to it. We need to create the best possible environment and best experience we can for them so that even developmental feedback is a positive experience.

> **Tip:** Stop what else you're doing. Physically turn away from your desk and give the person your full attention. Establish eye contact.

## *Principle 7: Give direction*

This principle may be one that sounds obvious. Of course we need to give direction. We don't want to take away from the individuals though and their opportunity to think for themselves so you'll notice that this follows on from the principle of self-discovery.

Being a coach or a leader means that you need to ensure the individual goes away with something specific they can do. They don't just need encouragement – although that's important. If encouragement was all that was required, you could be a cheerleader instead of a team leader. Telling someone they're doing ok or that something wasn't too bad doesn't actually give them any help as to how to make it better or how to improve.

Let's take an example here. Say you were blindfolded and were trying to throw paper balls into a waste paper basket. If the person watching you just said things like: "Not bad", "Ohhh that was close", "Nice try", "Good". Does that actually tell you anything constructive towards getting the paper in the basket? Not really. It may sound encouraging and you may feel like you're on the right track but being on the right track isn't good enough if you really want to get the paper in the basket. You need phrases like: "Try it three inches to the left", "Just about an inch higher", you keep hitting the left hand rim". These phrases actually give you something to work with. They are directions.

Again, if you wanted to get somewhere specific, you would naturally ask directions (unless you're like me. In which case you will exhaust every possible hunch you have about where to go first!) When someone gives you directions, they give you specific instructions to follow. It's not a game of 'hot' and 'cold' – it's specific statements about where to go in order to reach a destination.

Likewise, while coaching, you need to ensure that your instructions are specific and direct and not ambiguous.

> **Tip:**  Avoid adjectives like 'nearly there'. Focus on specific instructions. Treat it like a recipe or a list of directions to go somewhere or how to operate a piece of equipment.

# Principle 8: Change their perspective

Sometimes people struggle to 'get it' from the customer perspective. You obviously get it. Why don't they? This is a common issue that's faced. Part of the problem with this principle is that people haven't experienced what the customer is experiencing and find themselves with absolutely no empathy for the situation at all. This is especially evident when young people are employed and are serving customers in areas that they have no experience in. Take for example power companies. A school leaver dealing with customers in a power company may have never paid a power bill, don't know why it costs so much and has no idea of budgeting for it.

It's important therefore to focus on something they will have some idea about or some relationship to. For example, if you're trying to get across a point about the way they spoke to a customer, you may try to turn things round a bit and ask: "If that customer was your mother, would you be happy with the way she was treated?" Or "If you were on your lunch break and waited 15 minutes in a bank queue only to hear the person in front of you at the counter talk about the weekend sport – would you be happy about that?"

The trick is to find a scenario that will allow them to tap into their way of thinking and turn it around. What would make sense to them? What is the equivalent in their language or their world?

A simple way to look at this is to role play with them. You take on the role of the company and let them be the customer. Then run a scenario similar to the one you are trying to get them to improve. Don't take any prisoners either. Help them see how unreasonable, difficult, crazy it may sound like to them.

**Tip:** Put the individual in the shoes of the customer or try to turn the customer into someone that they care about such as a family member or a good friend.

# Principle 9: Use positive language

Your staff will mimic you. I have noticed when videoing coaching sessions in the past that the person being coached ends up talking similarly to the person who is coaching. Sometimes, people actually start using the exact same words.

We want our staff to be confident and positive with our customers so we need to be examples of that when we are talking with them. There's no doubt that as customers we want to feel confident in the person who we are speaking with. Imagine what it would be like if we asked our insurance company if something was covered under the policy and they replied, "I think so" or "It should be". Those types of responses do not create a feeling of safety or peace of mind. We expect to hear things like "Yes it does" or "No it doesn't, but it does cover you for xxx".

Imagine if you went to the doctors and you were given some medication and you asked if it would help with a particular ailment and all you got was the doctor shrugging their shoulders. You just wouldn't bother taking the medication would you? What would be the point?

Some of the words that we use don't support the positive, confident environment we want to portray. Avoid using words like, 'should, maybe, possibly, perhaps'. All these words leave questions about the situation. Some people try to soften sentences by using these words as preambles. Just don't do it. Be confident. One great way to improve on this yourself is to practice. Record yourself and listen to the types of words you use. These 'wishy washy' words often come out when we are in a conflict situation and would rather not be. It may take a little time to eradicate them in your coaching sessions and the best way is to be conscious of them. Listen to yourself and catch yourself when you say them. Of course – they may be necessary in some instances. I've just used the word 'may' twice in this paragraph. Just make sure that they're used correctly and not thrown in for good measure.

---

**Tip:**    Make a list of negative sounding words and practice not using them. Work on words you can use as substitutes.

---

## *Principle 10: Keep it simple*

It's the old adage of K.I.S.S. – keep it simple stupid. The more we load up our staff, the less likely they are of completing any of it. Think about trying to keep a shopping list in your head. By the time you get to the supermarket – it's gone or morphed into some other list. If you're anything like me, by the time you've ended your shop, your basket or trolley is full of stuff not on your original list. The brain just doesn't work well with keeping lists of things to do but works very well when there are just one or two things to focus on.

When you're coaching someone, there may be a list of 10 or 12 things that they need to work on. Forget it. That's just not practical. Get them to focus on the one or two things that will make the biggest impact in their role or to their performance. The likelihood is that if they fix those things, some of the others will fall into place as a result anyway. If the list of areas to work on is too long, they will just not know where to start. It's best to fix a couple of things, get them embedded then work on a couple more.

> **Tip:**   When you have your list of things for the person to work on, pick 1, 2 or 3 things at the most that will make the biggest impact for them and the business. Look for a quick win where you can. It will encourage them to do more.

— —

# Formal coaching

Planned coaching with an agenda will create some security and parameters for the individual being coached. It's important to set the expectation in these sessions so people are comfortable and not surprised. Try to set them at ease. Let them know in advance of what will take place wherever possible. Remember, you want those being coached to get something from this session. You want an improvement in behaviours. You want them to look forward to it so they need to see what's in it for them.

You may like to consider the following five steps in a formal coaching session:

1. Introduction

2. Agenda building

3. Discussion

4. Action point/plan

5. Summary

## 1. Introduction

Begin with a clear statement of why you are meeting

*"Our meeting today is your (1st, 2nd, 3rd) discussion for this year…."*

Then go on to outline what you will be doing.

*"We will be reviewing the progress you are making towards…..
and how you are using the coaching to help you achieve your*

*customer service standards. It will mean looking at what you need to continue to do, do more of and stop doing…"*

Follow this with a description of how you will conduct the discussion.

*"We start by setting the agenda. We have one hour, and need to ensure we cover all the issues important to each of us. Once we've decided our agenda we'll discuss each item in turn. I'd like your views first and then I will give my views. After a good discussion we'll agree whatever action needs taking and record the action points. I'd like you to record those and then summarise them at the end. That way, we can be sure that we agree on what has been discussed and what each of us needs to do. After the meeting I'll need a copy of the action points"*

## 2. Agenda Building

Try drafting in advance of the session. Don't forget to review action points from your last coaching session.

If you haven't reviewed the previous coaching session, make sure it is completed before starting the discussion.

*"Let's start by building the agenda. What topics or issues do you have? (They list them) I'd like to talk about ……….. plus……….."*

If the agenda is a long one, you might have to set some priorities in order to manage them.

*"It looks as if we may have more here than we can deal with right now. I would definitely like to cover…what are your priority items? Ok then we'll talk about…plus the others if we have time. Otherwise we'll set another meeting."*

## 3. Discussion

With each item on the agenda ask for your staff member's views first. With an open question invite them to, for example, talk about what they've been particularly pleased with.

Ask questions and probe for further clarification before giving your views. Once you understand their views, ask for suggestions and actions.

Explore important issues – give them the necessary time

Make sure that you give positive feedback when you can. *"I particularly liked the way you ...."*

Don't avoid problems. Take a joint problem solving approach. Analyse what happened and why things happened, without judging. What learning needs to take place from the problem?

What action points are needed for improvement?

Use the competencies to suggest how things could be done differently.

*"The problem we've identified links directly to these categories in the performance standards. Taking more time to ........."*


## 4. Action Points

Ensure that each agenda item results in action and that the staff member records this.

*"What do you think you need to do to make sure that doesn't happen again? Make a note that I need to provide you........."*

Action points should be concise, relevant and easy to apply. You could use the acronym:

**SMART:**

**Specific** – actual statements of what needs to happen eg: *"On each phone call with the customer, I will ask their permission to ask the validation questions as a lead in rather than just asking them with no introduction."*

**Measurable** – We will review this in our phone call observations each week and see if it's happening

**Achievable** – You have received the training and know how to do it

**Relevant** – This will help you in your role and make an impact on both your performance and the experience of the customer

**Time Bound** – You will start immediately and we will check on it weekly

Together these points form the action plan – which is then available for monitoring at the next performance discussion.


## 5. Summary

At the end of the discussion phase, ask the staff member to summarise.

Use the summary to ensure that the action points are clear and agreed to by you both.

Identify any leftover items or issues that need later discussion.

Remind the staff member to give you a copy of the action points.

70:30 discussion in coaching where you only do the 30% of the talking as the coach – remember the key element of self-discovery.

It's important not to cancel scheduled coaching sessions. Doing so sends a signal that the individual is less important than whatever activity or person has 'bumped' them off the schedule. Try everything you can to follow through on planned coaching sessions.

**Advantages of Formal Coaching:**

- It's scheduled so it should happen

- It's planned so there is a structure to follow

- It's regular, so follow up is built in and scheduled

- There are parameters set so expectations are easy to understand

- You should be away from the working area so it's easier to both give full attention

**Tip:** Schedule a formal coaching session at a time that suits both you and the person being coached. Never cancel a coaching session.

—— ——

# Informal coaching

Unlike formal coaching, informal coaching can be done anytime and anywhere. It's normally impromptu or casual in its set up. We may still have a set time to sit with our teams or to 'walk the floor' but we may not have a series of things to mention, bring up or discuss. Informal coaching is not about correcting mistakes. How much nicer would environments at work be if we tried to catch people 'doing things right' rather than the usual 'correct mistakes'.

Informal coaching can have a greater impact than formal coaching because it is immediate. If you consider the time / impact curve as displayed earlier in the book and below, the shorter the time has elapsed, the greater the impact is on the outcome. The longer you wait to comment on someone's behaviour, the less the impact will be. If you can say to someone immediately after a great sales call or a fantastic customer interaction that they did a terrific job, it will mean more than when you mention something in a formal meeting two weeks later.

Informal coaching can happen anytime. By its very name, informal means that there will unlikely be a regular set of rules or guidelines. Coaching of this nature can happen just about anytime, anywhere. You don't need (and probably shouldn't) start a conversation of informal coaching by mentioning anything about coaching. It's normally best to happen in the flow of a conversation or in the spontaneous moment.

You can informally coach someone as you walk past their desk, or as you walk the floor generally, as you leave a sales call with them, as you chat over the water cooler, as you talk in the elevator or as they come to your office about something. The good thing about this is that there are no real rules. Use the techniques described earlier in the book under the 10 Key Principles of Coaching.

**Advantages of Informal Coaching:**

- It's brief and requires little or no planning

- You can correct mistakes instantly and avoid them being repeated

- It's immediate and has a far greater impact than a delayed response

- It can be done anytime, anywhere

- Doesn't have to be done under the banner of 'coaching'

- It can be totally impromptu

**Tip:** Use informal coaching opportunities to reinforce good behaviour and catch people 'doing things right'.

—  —

# Remote employees

Sometimes you may find yourself in a position where geographically, you will not be able to effectively lead and coach in the physical space. You may have team members spread far and wide and need to engage in different methods for engaging them.

Ensure that you still make time for these employees to make small talk and build rapport. You can do this by phone and email and of course through video mediums. Ensure that you schedule longer 'one on one' sessions with remote staff as they don't benefit from the regular everyday association as you might see in an office environment.

Avoid cancelling 'one on one' sessions at all cost. This should be true for any staff member but is particularly harmful for remote employees. They already miss out on the informal contact, so show them you value the scheduled contact enough not to cancel it. The message it sends is one of lack of respect for them or at the very least that they are of lesser value than others or other tasks.

When you do schedule meetings remotely, try to balance the inconvenience for all parties. That means that if you are spread over different time zones, try to have the meetings at different times showing that you are willing to be up late or get up early!

Another great way to help them feel included and valued is to send them company 'swag' for them and their families. Help them feel like they are part of the wider team by sending them t-shirts, caps and other company merchandise and provide some for their families. It will help to feel like their family is part of the company team too.

If your staff members engage with customers on the phone, then remote coaching can be a great way to see how they perform using that medium. You can identify if they are prepared or easily distracted and unlike scenarios you may role play with them face to face, you are focusing on their tone and voice elements much more which can be very useful if the telephone is the method they use to perform their task.

In any event, knowing a few key skills on remote coaching can help in your role – especially if you don't want to have to wait until the next time you are physically meeting with someone to offer feedback or to coach them. This is very useful if you need to address something that needs immediate attention. Don't neglect the other skills discussed in this book. They are all relevant while coaching remotely.

There are several mediums for remote coaching including the telephone, video conferencing, Skype, Instant Messenger, Facetime, Internet meeting programmes etc. Video conferencing and video Skype options give you the benefit of seeing and hearing the other person. Some 'internet chat' options can drastically reduce the effectiveness of the communication as you lose both the physical language (unless you have a camera or web cam attached) and the audio language components. Look back at the chapter on communication to see how this can drastically affect the meaning of a sentence.

Remote coaching on the telephone can sometimes be easier in some respects. Some people find it easy to develop rapport and even trust on the telephone as it's a tool people use a lot of in their lives. It's important though not to slip into too much of an informal mode. You can lose some of the key elements of a good coaching session by treating a phone conversation as less important. Remember to consider having an agenda, a set time to talk, items to discuss and two-way communication. Always take the opportunity to follow up with an email to confirm actions and details of the conversation.

Ensure that you use a headset or some hands free operation. This leaves you free to takes notes and write things down, refer to notes etc. Don't try to hold a coaching session on the phone while you're driving though. It's potentially dangerous and at the very least you will be distracted and lose out on some of your key listening skills. It's obvious too that you shouldn't be 'multitasking' yourself and trying to check texts and emails etc while you're coaching someone on the phone. You need to be 'present' and concentrating on the person and your conversation.

As you aren't able to 'see' body language, your speaking and listening skills are more important in these settings. Ensure that you both paraphrase and encourage paraphrasing to confirm understanding. You can also develop the skill of 'hearing' the body language of the other person. You can hear if the person is being animated in their speech, if they are waving their arms around, smiling, tutting or even eating while they're in conversation with you.

Ensure that you allow silences to happen. It sounds more awkward on the telephone than face to face but you need to allow the other person time to think. You may have the experience yourself when someone explains something to you and asks immediately afterwards – "Well, what do you think?" Of course, you were listening right up until that point and then you're supposed to give an answer without processing it. Well we need time to process information, so allow those silences to happen.

You can continue to use the ten key points of coaching explained earlier. They are all still valid in remote coaching. Giving feedback, helping the other person self-discover and do most of the talking etc are all important elements of coaching, whether it's remote or face to face.

Finally, even though distance and travel may be a barrier to regular face to face meetings, ensure that you meet face to face at least annually (more frequently if possible). It's tough to work remotely and your team members need to feel they are part of something bigger, so help that message get across.

> **Tip:** Give remote employees extra attention. Send them more company 'swag' and schedule longer one-on-ones.

— —

# Barriers to coaching

There may be some objections raised by staff to coaching. Some are quite valid from their perspective, so it's a good idea to be armed with some good counter reasoning in order to solve and overcome the barriers.

Here are some of the barriers to coaching and potential solutions in dealing with them:

| Barrier | Solution |
| --- | --- |
| **Age (you may be younger than them)** | Get them on your side. Acknowledge that you value their experience in the organisation or life. Offer to receive feedback as well as give it. Ask for their help. Explain that although you're young, you have studied, practiced, learnt, researched – whatever it is you have done to deserve the role you're in. |
| **Age (you may be older than them)** | Acknowledge that you are of an older generation and your views on things may differ – especially preferences in music etc. Play to your strengths. You have a wealth of experience. You've made mistakes and learnt a lot. You bring stability, experience and knowledge. |

| Barrier | Solution |
|---|---|
| **Never been coached** | Ask them to share what they would like to get out of coaching. Reassure them that it's a positive experience. Share what you have gained from being coached and why you like to coach. Explain that coaching is where improvements happen and the benefits to them. |
| **New to the company** | Although you're new to the company, you bring with you specific leadership / coaching skills that qualify you for this role. Ask for their help in getting to understand the company products / services / systems etc. You were hired for your coaching and leadership skills, not for your company knowledge. |
| **No action** | Here's where the person says all the right things but doesn't change. Put in small, quick measures of accountability. Shorten the time span and follow up soon after. Ask the hard questions – "You said you would do this, why haven't you?" Don't offer excuses for them. Ensure they come up with the actions – don't set the measures – let them do it. |

| Barrier | Solution |
|---|---|
| **Repeated poor behaviour** | Ensure they have had adequate training and opportunities to practice. Go back to looking at the cause for the behaviour. Put in positive consequences for improvements and, negative consequences for continuing poor behaviour. Ask them to give reasons for the behaviour. Ask them what they would do if they were in your shoes and had to deal with them. |

— —

# Dealing with difficult behaviours

People naturally have a defence mechanism built into them commonly known as the 'fight or flight' response. It's that moment when you make a split decision to either fight and make a stand or run away to fight another day. Although our process time to think things through may have provided us with a different (and sometimes better) response, our immediate 'under pressure' response can be quite out of character and even damaging.

This response is caused by what's known as the amygdala hijack which is a term attributed to Daniel Goleman in his 1996 book "*Emotional Intelligence: Why It Can Matter More Than IQ*". In the book, the term is used to describe emotional responses from people which are out of measure with the actual threat because it has triggered a much more significant emotional threat. In other words, the emotional reaction to what is in front of you has triggered something of greater emotional importance. Often we hear of people 'over reacting' and that is often due to their emotional understanding of a particular event being greater than our own.

The main types of responses can be put into three categories: fight, flight and freeze. When coaching someone and especially while giving feedback, people already put themselves in a higher emotional state. The things that are spoken of hit personal registers and put people under pressure so you can often come up against the following:

**Fight response**

Some people tend to get angry or argumentative. They may stop listening or demonstrate other stubborn traits and may even get sarcastic. A 'Fight' response to these behaviours may include:

"Don't speak to me like that!" or

"If you don't calm down I'll terminate the call"

## Flight response

In this type of response, people tend to want to avoid conflict, blame someone else, blame a system fault, or pass the buck in general. Responses in a 'Flight' nature might include:

"One of the others must have told you that"

"It's not my problem"

"So you want to talk to the manager, then?"


## Freeze response

Here's where your mind goes blank, you can't think of anything to say or you feel embarrassed. The thing about the amygdala hijack is that it's automatic but we can control it. While our brain (cortex) is accessing its records for an appropriate response, the amygdale also receives the information and offers a shortcut immediate threat response and blocks off the 'slow thinking'. Our response to a situation will affect the outcome. If we think of the outcome in these terms: Outcome = Event + Response or written the other way: Event (E) = my response to the event, (R) = the outcome, then we know that:

E – things that will happen

R – how I choose to respond to it

O – will determine the outcome or result


As an example: If a staff member calls me names (E) and I get offended and shout back at them (R), then the outcome (O) is going to be conflict between us.

But...

If a staff member calls me names (E) and I ignore the name calling, keep calm and stick to the facts (R), then the outcome is going to be a more logical and productive discussion between us (O). So, how I manage my response or reaction to things and people can determine the end result I want to get. It all sounds straight forward and actually is. The simple four step process to remember in each case of potential conflict is:

1. Pause
2. Listen and acknowledge the response or the behaviour
3. Return to the facts
4. Focus on a solution

Here are a few examples of what can happen and how using this approach can assist. Let's take it that you are giving someone feedback on getting to work late:

| Event | Response |
|---|---|
| **Staff member cries** | 1. PAUSE<br><br>2. The aim of this discussion is not to upset you...<br><br>3. We are here to talk about the fact that you have been getting to work late<br><br>4. Tell me why this is happening? |
| **Staff member is aggressive** (e.g. says something like: you are such a bad manager) | 1. PAUSE<br><br>2. This discussion is not about me...<br><br>3. We are here to talk about the fact that you have been getting to work late<br><br>4. We need to agree how you are going to manage to get to work on time. |

| Event | Response |
|---|---|
| **Staff member is defensive** (e.g. why are you picking on me?) | 1. PAUSE<br><br>2. I am not picking on you...<br><br>3. The fact is, you have got to work more than 10 minutes late on the last 3 days<br><br>4. Tell me why this is happening? |
| **Staff member blames** (e.g. I'm not the only one in the team who is doing it) | 1. PAUSE<br><br>2. If it is happening with others, you can know that I will address it with them. Or what happens in other managers departments is not my issue. In this department, I expect my staff to get to work on time.<br><br>3, We are here to talk about your lateness, so...<br><br>4. Tell me why this is happening? |
| **Staff member is silent** | 1. PAUSE<br><br>2. If you don't talk to me, we cannot work together to fix it...<br><br>3. As I mentioned, you have been late the last 3 days.<br><br>4. Why is that? |

So, what we can see from these examples is that in each case, you can manage the response by:

1. Pausing (to manage the amygdala hijack)

2. Not taking things personally (reminding yourself that it was an attempt to divert your attention)

3. Sticking to the facts

4. Keeping the conversation moving forward to a solution.

**Tip:** Practice the four step process when difficult behaviours are exhibited: Pause, acknowledge, return to facts and focus on a solution.

—   —

# Dealing with conflict

As a leader, managing conflict is part of your role. It comes with the territory and you can use conflict that exists as a positive in your team. Don't be afraid of conflict. In basic terms, conflict can be a difference of opinion. It's healthy and helps to innovate and create ideas. Avoidance of conflict is often the topic that people discuss. A lot of people would rather avoid conflict than deal with it, because they only see the negative effects.

Some people don't stand up for their beliefs or their opinions and this only serves to have a group of people that say 'yes' to their leader or others and then the opportunity for improvement, tweaking, discussion and change is often lost. When you have a group that feels like they can't offer opinions or agree on what to do, they then complain about the decision later on. You then have a dissention issue which is often harder to fix. Conflict handled well, means people don't get hurt and don't take things personally. It's your role to ensure that you don't harm these relationships.

Set a clear expectation that it is okay to have a differing opinion and that a healthy debate can lead to a more defined and agreed outcome. Encourage others to speak up and express their opinion. Help them see the benefits of this. When it's time to agree or move forward with a decision then you can sum up, acknowledge the opinions and share the reasons for any decision that's been arrived at. Thank those who have offered opinions. Don't shoot people down in public for sharing ideas. Examine your own behaviours and see if you encourage opinions or somehow shut them down instead.

It's always useful to have others support their opinions with facts or data. This will help you in resolving conflicts between people if you can get them to recognise that the facts are the starting point. Supporting information is a great way to illuminate a problem. Get used to asking a question like, "What are the reasons for you coming to that conclusion?"

When encouraging opinions in your team, help the team understand that personal attacks are not tolerated. If people feel that there is equality, fairness and safety in expressing thoughts and opinions, you will get much more impact and variety as well as happier staff. You can train your staff in conflict handling and problem solving skills.

## Understand the type of conflict

Conflict situations can be of various types and include:

- Functional conflict: This is a disagreement with plans, policies or procedures

- Role-based conflict: This is a disagreement over the role someone is in or asked to perform

- Emotional conflict: This type of conflict involves basic feelings of anger, frustration, fear, jealousy etc.

It's important to identify the type of conflict before trying to sort it out. For example, if you try to fix someone's emotions that are actually being caused by a functional conflict, the resolution will be short lived. You will need to correct the functional issue first. Make sure that whatever you come up with as a solution doesn't have any road blocks to prevent it being successful.


## Methods of dealing with conflict in your team

Don't meet with antagonists separately. Allowing each person to individually share their views will only strengthen and polarise each position. They will see it as imperative that you understand their position and side with them. Meet with them together. Allow them to summarise and briefly share their views without the other party interrupting. If there are personal attacks, intervene.

Consider your role as a facilitator. Practice asking questions of those in the conflict that make them think about their position such as:

"What are the reasons for you proposing that?"

"Can we find a way to do this without criticizing each other personally?"

"What could you do to change?"

"What can you do more of, less of, start doing?"

"What impact do you think your behaviour has on the rest of the team?"

"What will you do next time this happens?"

"Can you explain that to me in a different way?"

"If we can't' agree, what will the consequences be?"

Come up with some questions of your own that help the people involved see that you want to help and that you expect them to come up with a solution that will work. It's not about asking them to shake hands and make up; it's about coming to an understanding on both sides and seeing the middle ground - a win-win if you like.

You can ask them to describe specific actions they would like the other to take with reasons for requesting those actions. For example, "I'd like Peter to give me the weekly data from the team by Thursday at 5pm so I can produce the report by Friday lunchtime." Help them commit to noticing that the other person has made a change, even if it is small. This is helping to acknowledge the effort of the other person.

Let them know that you will not choose sides and that you expect them to sort out the conflict as adults. If they refuse, explain that you will need to take it further which could lead to disciplinary action (always check with your HR representative first). Be sure that you always follow official processes.

Reassure them that you have every confidence in their ability to resolve the issue. Record the agreements and always set a time to review.

Be prepared to say no. Set some boundaries. Don't let people get away with saying things that are just not fair or are out of line and always ensure there are no personal attacks. If one person is out on their own with an opinion, you can ask if anyone else feels the same way. If they don't then maybe you have a strong case for moving on, claiming that they are the only ones with a diverse view. Thank them for it and move on.

Some conflict situations will highlight that someone is potentially in the wrong role and you may need to rethink positions, roles, responsibilities and relationships. Remember the old adage, if you can't change the people, change the people. If people just won't improve, alter their behaviours or be willing to compromise, then maybe it's time to move them out.

In any conflict situation, you must deal with it. You can't hope that it goes away. Deal with it quickly. Remind people about team charters, company objectives, the company's vision and mission – anything that will help those involved see that their behaviour is not in line with established procedures or policy.

**Tip:** In conflict, you don't come up with the solution, you help the antagonists arrive at a win-win position and leave with a shared understanding.

—— ——

# Dealing with bad attitudes

Bad attitudes in the workplace are a pain. As a manager, you may find yourself complaining about them to others and wish they'd just go away but how much of it is down to you? Attitudes of staff members may deteriorate due to a number of reasons, so to avoid them in the first place or help turn them round, have a look at the following.

**Be Fair**

Look at how you work with your staff. Are they paid fairly? Do you treat them well and avoid showing favouritism? Staff will quickly develop resentment when fairness is not apparent in the workplace.

**Listen**

Do you listen to your staff? Most people want to feel like they are contributing. Ask them for their opinions. At times, show that you are acting on their suggestions and they will feel more integrated and important.

**Communicate**

Let your staff know what is happening. Don't keep them in the dark. Tell them what's going on in the business; share the plans, the feedback from customers and upper management.

**Thank**

Let them know that you appreciate them. Small courtesies like 'Thank you' are often overlooked but can go a long way to build trust and improve morale. A little extra effort of showing appreciation on your part can help turn round or avoid the negative attitude of your staff.

## Steps to turn around bad attitudes

What you can do to help turn round existing bad attitudes is to follow these steps:

1. Note instances where their attitude has had a negative impact on work being completed or done well. Their attitude may have caused people to avoid them, which may have delayed a process. This could have caused a customer to miss out on a communication all because one of the team has not felt they were able to approach the person with the bad attitude. Record these instances so you can establish some facts.

2. Meet with the person that has the attitude and present your findings to them. Ask them to share their perspective. Just talking about it may help to dispel some of the issue. Stick to the facts so it is more difficult for them to argue.

3. Agree on what should happen as a result. Ask them to suggest what they can do to alter the situation. Get them to commit and follow up.

What you want to be able to do is reduce the reasons for someone to have a bad attitude, then if it happens, don't hope it goes away – act quickly because if you don't do something about it, you may lose the members of staff that you want to keep!

**Tip:** Keep an eye on what you are doing to ensure that you are not contributing to the bad attitudes of your staff – inconsistency of managers is one of the worst contributors to bad attitudes in the workplace.

—— ——

# Courageous conversations

There will definitely be times when you need to hold a difficult or courageous conversation. This basically means that you have a situation that needs addressing. There are some things that just don't go away, or get worse the longer you leave them. It's not just the natural consequences for leaving things, it's also the pressure that builds up in you personally and that can lead to stress and be a real problem for leaders.

Many people put off having difficult conversations. There are lots of reasons. It may be that we just fear the outcome. We don't want to hurt our relationship with the other person. Maybe we don't want to feel uncomfortable, deal with the emotions of the other person or perhaps we are just not sure what will happen, so we avoid it.

It may be that we are just feeling uncomfortable about something. Perhaps we're angry at someone, we're avoiding someone or something, we may be embarrassed or ashamed of something or just worried about the consequences of the conversation.

There are so many benefits from having the difficult conversation such as:

- The behaviour you're addressing can cease from that moment
- You can clear the air
- You can get more commitment from your staff members
- You feel less stressed
- People will trust and respect you more.

So, how do you start? Well, identify what it is that you're not 100% comfortable with – this is the dissatisfaction component of how we are feeling. We need to make sure what it is that's making us uncomfortable and make that the focus. Now identify what it is that we want or need to express to the other party. Imagine the worst outcome that could happen as a result of having the conversation and accept that possibility. Let go of the thing that is holding you back and remember it's okay to feel uncomfortable and focus on the fact that at least after the conversation you won't have those feelings of trepidation any more – they'll be gone because you will have addressed it.

When you address the person, you can explain to the person that you have some difficult feedback to share if you like. Brace them for what may be coming. You can even say that you feel uncomfortable about having to give the feedback. Avoid telling them that it's someone else who has brought it to your attention. You could even say that the situation demands that you give the feedback. Get to the point quickly and link the change you expect to a positive business impact and agree on an action.

Let's say you need to address a personal hygiene problem with another member of staff. So, you've identified that the issue does in fact exist and you need to address it with them. The bonus for you is that they may not be aware of the issue and might be very grateful to you for bringing it to their attention. That is the best outcome of the situation and does happen sometimes.

However, you have to get there first and it's always good to be direct and get to the point fast. You may say something to this person along the lines of:

> *"I need to discuss something with you that is awkward and uncomfortable for me. I do hope that I don't offend you. You have had a noticeable body odour lately and I wanted to bring it to your attention as most people wouldn't know this about themselves."*

I suggest you then follow up with something that you believe may be the reason or cause. For example, if you notice they wear the same clothes all week long, you can suggest that it may have something to do with that.

At this point you will know whether the person is embarrassed or goes on the offensive. You will notice that in the suggested wording above, you didn't mention that people had complained about them – that will only make things worse. You have stayed with the facts by saying they have a noticeable body odour. If they do take a stance and refuse to admit it, you can remain on the factual slant and tell them that they need to respect the workplace and come to work clean.

You may also point out other potential causes such as the list above and ask them to have a think about what they can do. Get them to commit to some action and make sure you follow up. Give yourself a reward task to do after dealing with the situation – you deserve it!

For any difficult or courageous conversation, you may like to follow the simple DESCCO steps. These steps were explained earlier as part of the ten principles of effective coaching and they are worth examining again for the purpose of having a courageous or difficult conversation. You can either follow the steps by explaining them yourself or by asking the other person to fill in each gap. It really does help to encourage self-discovery.

Here are the steps:

**D**escribe the behaviour

**E**xpress how you felt

**S**pecify what you'd prefer

**C**onsequences of the new action

**C**ontract to act in the new way

**O**k.

Firstly, if you wanted to give direct feedback to someone, say for complaining about everything you ask them to do, you might use it like this:

> "Peter, when you complain about my direction, I feel like you don't respect me as the leader of this team, I'd prefer it that if you don't agree with what I've asked, that you wait until you have an opportunity when you can address me personally, tell me why you don't like what you've heard and offer me an alternative. That way, you won't be disrupting everybody else and potentially distracting them in their work flow and together we may find a better solution. So, can I expect you to do that next time you feel like complaining in the group? Okay."

So, you'll see in that short paragraph that we used all the steps of DESCCO in a simple flow:

**Describe**:      "When you complain about my direction..."

**Express**:      "I feel like you don't respect me as the leader of this team."

**Specify**:      "I'd prefer it that if you don't agree with what I've asked, please wait until you have..."

**Consequences**:      "That way, you won't be disrupting everybody else and potentially distracting them in their work flow ..."

**Contract:**     "So, can I expect you to do that next time…"

**Ok:**     "Okay."

Each of the steps has an important element to play in helping people to alter their behaviour. Firstly, describing what they did helps the person know exactly what it is you're talking about. It's therefore much more useful if the feedback given is descriptive (i.e. factual). The expression component then personalises it and gives some meaning to the effect of their behaviour. Specifying another way of approaching it gives them an alternative and explaining the consequences (which could be good or bad) gives reasoning for the person to consider the new behaviour suggestion. The contract is a way of getting them to concur or show their understanding. The ending with 'Okay' is for them to agree.

In our example above, we have shown a direct 'telling' method of giving feedback. Of course, it can be even more powerful if you switch the 'telling' to 'asking' in each of the steps of the DESCCO process after the 'Describe' step. For example, "When you shouted across the office, what impact do you think that had on the rest of the team?" This way you will be able to uncover their understanding and thinking a lot sooner, and potentially gain greater buy-in.

You may need to have a difficult conversation on the phone, or when someone calls in sick. Maybe someone is away and decides to text you or email you. You really need to pick up the phone and hold the conversation. A difficult conversation is just that – it's a conversation. It's not a series of emails or texts.

There are lots of techniques you can try. You can even use the phrase, "If you were me, what would you do?" It's a great phrase to turn the tables and help the individual see things from your perspective.

There are many benefits for holding these conversations. In one particular organisation where there were four Team

Leaders, the team that had the lowest absenteeism was the team where the leader held these types of conversations. When a staff member was absent, they would telephone them and ask what help they needed. They didn't avoid the situation. The team responded with more effort and recognised their own need to be accountable.

One thing is for sure, the more you hold these conversations, the easier they become and your confidence increases.

**Tip:**   Always link the change you want to a positive impact it will have on the business. Help them see that by changing their behaviour, there will be a positive business impact.

— —

# Delegation

Some people use lots of excuses for not delegating. Usually, their reasoning has no actual basis of truth – they just think it does. You'll get a lot more accomplished if you don't assume the following statements are true and use them as excuses for not delegating:

- I don't have time to show them how to do it

- They are already busy

- They aren't properly qualified, I'm the only person who knows how to do this

- I could do a better job myself

- I can't trust them to do it

- No one else is available to delegate to

- They did a dreadful job last time

- I like doing all this stuff

We often spend time assuming the worst of people. We think they don't want to do what we ask them or that they just won't be up to the task. Consider changing your approach. Remember the Pygmalion effect from earlier on in the book. If we treat people like they can't do something or don't want responsibility, that's how they'll turn out.

Think about you personally, don't you want extra responsibility? People want to achieve, contribute and learn. They get all of these things by doing other tasks. Some short term investment in their development will pay off in the long term.

## *What can you delegate?*

The first thing to remember is not to delegate something that doesn't need doing. Why are you doing it in the first place? Just stop doing it.

Try to delegate the routine stuff, even if you would rather not. This could include photocopying, collecting information, entering data, preparation of reports etc.

Look to delegate things that aren't part of your core role or skill set. You can't be an expert at everything, so delegate out the stuff that takes you longer than other people.

If you think there's nothing you can delegate, what happens when you're on holiday or on sick leave or if you had to take an extended leave of absence – is everything going to pile up for you? The more you have the ability to delegate, the more you can enjoy a day or more away from the business. If there's absolutely something you can't delegate, then okay but try to keep that list as short as possible.

When you are delegating, have some sort of plan so your delegation isn't haphazard and remember that the responsibility still lies with you for getting the job done well and properly.

Remember that when you delegate something, someone may find a better way of doing it so you may learn something yourself or they may end up doing a better job than you.

## *Giving instructions*

When you are delegating, ensure that the instructions are clear. You should make sure the person you are delegating to knows what is to be done, when it should be finished by and to what degree of quality or detail.

Ask people to provide you with a progress report of how things are going. You may like to give them a cushion deadline where you have some extra time set aside just in case.

Consider delegating what the actual objective is rather than the procedure. People can get behind an outcome much more than they can the methodology for doing it.

Ensure you delegate the authority along with the responsibility. It can be really frustrating for someone to be delegated something to do but have no authority in the process. Give them the decision making power within boundaries you feel comfortable with.

Spread the delegation around. Don't always give things to the most able person and ask for feedback on how the tasks are going.

To help get the person going, ask the simple questions, "What else do you need to get started?" It's a great way for them to either tell you what help they need or for them to realise it's time to get a move on!

> **Tip:** Remember these three important factors and make sure the person to whom you are delegating understands what is to be done, when it should be finished by and to what degree of quality or detail.

— —

# Change management

In the business world, there is a constant flow of change. In fact, some industries are all about change. We have new technologies, restructures, new team members, new board members, changes in governments, new laws etc. Managing people through change is often difficult, especially if they know a change is coming but they're not sure what it is yet.

The biggest issue with change management being conducted poorly is lack of communication. People really just want to be kept informed for a start. The grapevine (the unofficial communication line) carries a majority of truth but is not often reliable. Companies that provide transparency are more likely to maintain a sense of loyalty in their staff.

Many people are resistant to change. In fact you may have resisted some change yourself. If change is resisted, it's normally something that has to be accepted at some point so you may be putting off the inevitable. As a leader, if change is coming, you need to get on board quickly so you can assist your team with getting on board.

A great book on change is "Who moved my cheese?" by Spencer Johnson. The book is simply a story about two mice and two people who are used to having cheese available in the same place every day. One day the cheese diminishes and eventually is gone altogether. The story follows the characters and their attitudes to this change. I highly recommend you read the book.

There are several messages in the book including the following:

- Change Happens. Accept the fact that change is part of life and things will change. We can't expect all things to remain constant or there will be no progress.

- Anticipate the change. Keep your eyes open. Things don't stay the same for very long. Be aware of what's going on around you and be prepared to move again. Don't allow yourself to be blindsided and catch you unaware.

- Monitor the change. It is hard to always be on the lookout for constant change – especially after change has just happened. However, monitoring the change to make sure it isn't going to change again without you knowing is important – it's like an extension of anticipating the change. Just keep looking and seeing how it's panning out.

- Adapt to change quickly. The quicker you adapt, the quicker you can embrace and enjoy the new change. Old habits and attitudes need to go when the new change comes in. If you cling onto these old habits and attitudes, you just make things difficult for those around you and yourself. You don't want to be the one who is always complaining about it not being like it used to be. When you consciously accept change, you find you just then get on with it and you can move on. It's only when we refuse to accept or just ignore the change that we find ourselves constantly 'swimming' against the tide – and it's really hard work!

- Move with the change. This requires effort and means that you run with the new change. You actually move in the direction of the change. Be a mover, not a passive spectator of change.

- Enjoy the change. Once it's happened, take time to enjoy it. If it's a new person moving in to a role – enjoy the fresh experience. If you have a new process to perform, take time to enjoy the new opportunity etc. If you keep being obstinate about the change you will never be able to enjoy it and the rest of your life. If you don't embrace the change and get the blessings of it, you will look at change as the enemy and something that will steal whatever enjoyment you could have had, that the change could bring.

- Be ready to change again. Positivity feeds on itself. If you have the right attitude no matter the circumstances, you will enjoy life so much more. So if change is running away from you, catch up to it and change your attitude towards it and enjoy life!

*Practical Leadership*                                             142

## *Embracing change*

In order to help yourself and other people move with the change you can focus on the following:

1. Seek to understand the change
2. Make a conscious decision to embrace the change
3. Identify the benefits of the change
4. Link the change to your own personal values
5. Accept that others may resist or struggle
6. Explore the perception of others about the change.

Let me explain a bit more about each of these points and how they can assist you in accepting and embracing the change and how you can then help others to do the same.

Seek to understand the change. For us to accept change, it helps to fully understand what it is and what it means for us. So many times, people assume what a change is and find it is something very different when it happens.

Consciously accept the change. When you make the decision to accept the change, it allows you to move on and move forward. Until you decide to accept the change, you will be using up a certain amount of energy in resistance to it.

Look for benefits in the change. Sometimes it's hard. If the change is a reduction in salary due to cut backs, you may find it difficult to find benefits. One may be that at least you still have a job. Finding benefits helps to focus on what to look forward to as a result of the change. It gives you focus and a positive link.

Link the change to your personal drivers or values. If you can find a link in the change that matches your own personal drivers, again you will find a very good focus to put your energies into.

Accept that others may struggle with the change. If you can change or move with the change because you have identified certain benefits or established some good links, it doesn't mean that everyone else has. Be patient with others and accept that it may take a while longer for them to get on board.

Ask others what they are thinking about the change. Explore options with them. Ask them how it will affect them, have they identified any benefits themselves.

## *Help others accept change*

Once you have managed all this for yourself, it's time for you to help your team do the same. You may like to run a short workshop to help them go through these processes themselves and help them manage this change process. Help them identify benefits, link to personal drivers and understand the change.

Sell the benefits of the change to others and if you feel like it, become a champion of the change. Be someone who is an example of the change benefits and what they mean.

Part of the leader's role is to manage change and help others through it and the best way to do that is to become converted to the change yourself. You may need to take some time out and follow the six steps above so you can internalise the correct attitude and be ready to help others experience the same for themselves. Remember the longer you resist the change, the less happiness you will find.

**Tip:** Focus on the benefits of the change and link your personal drivers. Once you are committed, you are better placed to help others.

—— ——

# Recruitment, on-boarding and training

As a leader, you will undoubtedly be involved in these three activities. For each, it's important to have a plan. To have a plan, you need to be aware of the organisational strategy, so it's important to be informed. Being informed is not passive. To 'be informed' means that you are the one to ensure you are up to date. You can do this by proactively networking in your organisation and staying in the loop. Get a feel for what is supposed to happen. Does your business hire people on contract or permanently? Do you have a centralised induction or on-boarding team? Who is responsible for the ongoing training budget?

You can talk to peers in other businesses to find out what works best in your field.

These three areas are linked together. You recruit someone whose first 90 days determine if they stay and how much training they may need ongoing.

## *Recruitment*

It's important to know what you really need by way of human resources. What characteristics are you looking for? Are you going to recruit on skills and experience or will you train on those areas and look for people with a great attitude? If you get your recruitment process right, you can save a lot on training and further recruitment.

Whether you use an agency or do all recruitment processes in-house, ensure that you don't oversell the opportunity. There's no point getting someone on board only to lose them in the first 90 days because they feel like they are working in a different place to what you explained to them. When one of the shipping docking companies realised that their crane operators were walking out during induction, they changed their recruitment process to include a trip up one of the cranes. Right there and then it eliminated those that couldn't handle the height. This previously had not featured until they had employed the person.

Culturally too, ensure you understand what happens during the interview process. I personally had an experience while interviewing for production staff. A lady came to the interview with an older lady who I assumed was there for moral support. The lady interviewed well and I told her to start the following Monday. Only when the start of the week arrived did I realise I'd employed her mother!

Working with a recruitment consultant will cost money but may save you in the long run. Do you know how much it actually costs to replace someone in your team? Consider the following:

- Advertising the role
- Recruitment agency fees
- Time sifting through CVs
- Interviewing
- Position description work
- Loss of productivity while someone is not there
- Loss of knowledge from those who have left
- Speed to competency of new people
- Actual training costs
- Reduction in morale of other staff
- Additional workload

Some businesses actually equate the retraining cost of a new staff member to equal their annual salary. It's important then to get the right person on board as well as motivating them to stay and perform well through your fabulous practical leadership skills!

## *On-boarding and induction*

You may have a centralised team looking after this. Even if you have, make sure you have some input. Help the new person have a great first 90 day experience. This is when most new people decide the new job is not for them.

One of the best ways to plan an induction programme is to layer the experience. Avoid putting all of the same topics together. For example, consider scheduling some systems and process stuff in the morning and do some service related training or role plays in the afternoon. Break up the experience so that the new person gets a little of everything each day or at least every two days. If you do a week of company policy followed by a week of systems work then a day of soft skills training, you may find that they have forgotten all the policy stuff by week three anyway.

Consider making the induction process as short as possible and the practical buddying up or early days stretched out a bit. Train people on how to find what they need rather than to memorise everything.

Having people start their roles sooner builds confidence. If the role is complicated, get them started quickly but on some simple tasks first. As they grow in confidence, add more tasks on top. This way, their contribution to the business is almost happening from day one and their 'real' experience is building right from the start.

Get them to meet other teams in the business quickly. Help them see where they fit in and the impact their role will have on the wider business as well as the customers.

## *Training*

You could consider training to include coaching. Formal training may happen when they are in a classroom or out of their official role. This should happen when you need them to learn new skills. Remember, people don't need training if they know how to do something. If they aren't doing it, they need motivation. Don't mix the two up, as you will be wasting your time.

Training doesn't fix everything. Consider the individual. Ask the question, 'What does this person need to be able to do this task?' Training should be reserved for when someone doesn't know how to do something. Coaching or buddying up is when someone knows (or should know) how to do something but needs some improvement or more opportunities for practice.

Consider refresher training for tasks or areas that are more infrequent or where people have fallen into bad habits. This may be particularly relevant in soft skills areas (e.g. how to deliver great customer service) or in hard skills (e.g. using machinery) when the need is infrequent or you have noticed a drop in performance. They may simply have not had to do something for a while and forgotten, or they may have so much to remember they can't store it all. Coaching can usually fix this if done regularly, but for consistency and for an opportunity to build team spirit, consider refresher training.

Have a plan for training. Over the year, what competencies do your people need to be proficient in? Can you plan and calendar sessions in advance? Can you handle training in-house or do you need a professional service firm to come in and assist you?

Speaking of these areas together again, one business once shared with me that their annual budgets were $20,000 for training and $180,000 for recruitment. Taking into account the fact their headcount was not growing or diminishing overall, they were spending far too much on recruiting people rather than on keeping good people.

In summary, consider how you have these three areas structured and are you happy with the way they are being implemented. If some of the process is out of your hands and you would like to change something, you can suggest to the appropriate people what you think. Don't throw your hands in the air and say it's out of your hands. Start to influence what you can and drive change yourself.

**Tip:** Whatever internal resources you have, get involved and help with the planning and execution of these areas.

— —

# Set clear expectations

One of the big issues that people have with their managers is that they claim their manager changes their mind or moves the goalposts. All frustration is born out of unmet expectations. Not just people with their bosses. ANY frustration is as a result of not having your expectations met. If you expect one thing and get another, you get frustrated (unless of course your expectation is exceeded)!

So, think about your communication with your team. Make sure it's clear and concise. Avoid ambiguity unless you intend for it to be there. Remember the components for clear delegation; what is it you want done? When do you want it done by? To what standard and quality should it be completed? If you are clear, neither party will be disappointed or frustrated.

## *Consultation*

One area of clear frustration is in consultation. If you are asked for your opinion on something and then someone totally ignores you, you wonder why they bothered asking you in the first place. Well, your team will be the same. If your intention is to gather opinions but make the decision yourself then tell them, so they don't get the wrong idea.

There are three types of consultation, namely:

- We'll discuss – I'll decide: This is where you talk things over with your team or the stakeholders involved, but you retain the entire decision making process. You may canvass their opinions and they may influence your ultimate decision but you may still run with your original thoughts. In this case, you must tell your people at the outset that this is your intention. Let them know that you will ultimately make the decision but you value their opinion.

- We'll discuss – we'll decide: As the phrase suggests, this is decision-making based on true consensus. Here you work with your team to come up with a decision. Ensure that everyone has their say and is heard. For those who don't normally say a lot or contribute, give them some advance notice about the topic because they may be the kind of person that likes to think things through before talking. As a leader you may miss out on some valuable insights because of this fact.

- We'll discuss – you'll decide: This version means that you are inviting others to consult with you but you're not offering to make the decision for them. You may offer advice and ideas but the decision is theirs and they have the responsibility too.

## Brainstorming

Gather your team's ideas through brainstorming. You can do this effectively with a whiteboard or flipchart. You can pose a question or a statement and then canvass ideas. While brainstorming, it's important not to throw anything out to start with. The minute you shoot someone down for an idea, everyone will feel uncomfortable because they don't want to get the same treatment.

Your goal here is to get everyone to contribute as much as possible. You can reduce the list of ideas afterwards. You can improve your chances of fresh thinking by using methodologies like LEGO Serious Play or an external facilitator. Use open and searching questions to get people started and thinking.

Always provide feedback to your team following their involvement. One of the biggest complaints about managers is that they ask for their team's opinions and thoughts and that's the last anyone hears about the subject. Ensure you feedback to them the result and updates along the way. They will appreciate it.

## Clarification

One of the simplest errors in communication is the failure to clarify. It's a great practice and easy to do once the habit is formed. Train your team to clarify with you to ensure they are clear with your instructions. Help them see the importance of clarification by doing it yourself. If there is any doubt, check. It only takes a minute and can save hours of wasted time and effort or correction of mistakes and embarrassment in the long run.

You want your customers to have a great experience and you don't want them to experience errors or problems. Many of these can be overcome by having your team clarify with them their requests or needs. If they get used to doing it with you, they'll do it with the customers and vice versa. Highlight mistakes that are caused because of the lack of clarification. Show how easy it would have been to avoid the error if they had clarified.

> **Tip:** Get used to asking clarifying questions. Train your team to do the same. With clear expectations and less ambiguity, you'll have less disappointment.

— —

# Power questions and power phrases

Barrack Obama as US President once stated that one of the key skills effective leaders of the future will have is their ability to ask powerful questions. It is true that transformational leaders – those that wish to transform change in others, ask innovative and searching questions and lots of them. So whether it's a question or a phrase you want to share with your team, consider how you can make it powerful.

As an example, if one of your staff members is consistently late to work, you may be tempted to ask a factual question such as, "Why were you late today?" There's nothing wrong with that question, but it isn't very soul searching. You may get a factual response like, "I overslept" or, "I missed the bus" but that's about as far as you may get. Consider the alternative, "What impact do you think you being late has had on the rest of the team?" With this question, you have suddenly transformed the emphasis away from the reason they may have been late to the impact it has had on other people.

A powerful question is one that makes the person we ask to think or to search their soul. Consider the self-posed powerful question, "Why do I do what I do?" Occasionally, we should all take a minute and ask ourselves this question. "Why do I do it?" It helps to focus our efforts and remind us as to why we're in business.

We often get so wrapped up in everything we do that our tasks meld into one and we can get caught up in mundane tasks very easily, so consider the important question, "Is what I am doing now the most important thing I can be doing with my time?" Wow! What a great question. In fact, ask it of yourself right this moment. What's the answer? Is there something else you could be doing that would have more impact in your role or your life right now?!

So consider a few powerful questions or phrases you can keep and refer to with your team, so that you can help them be more likely to understand a deeper purpose or reason for doing something. Here are a few other power phrases and power questions you could consider using:

- Why do we do it that way?
- Would that behaviour be acceptable if it was your mother calling?
- Own it!
- Make this one really count.
- Imagine this is the last call you will ever take. How would you like it to go?
- What would make this perfect?
- What would happen if we changed this?
- How long do you think we could last without customers?
- What's the one thing you would change if there was no limit?
- What's stopping you?

Questioning is pretty basic in the communication cycle but we still don't always use effective questioning. It's true that open and closed questions are the basic types of questioning but there is so much more to communicating than that. When I ask my children how their day went, it doesn't matter if I ask an open or closed question; I still get a one word answer like "Stuff" or a shoulder shrug. One of the better ways I have found to get them to open up (which is what we want from our team members) is to rephrase the question in to more of a request, "Tell me about your day". It gives them less of an option to avoid talking. Try it out. Use "Tell me about that conversation" or "Tell me about that customer" rather than "What was that conversation like?"

When you are talking with your team members, be ready to challenge them. It's part of your job to help them find the understanding as to why things are done, why customers need what they do, why your business exists. We need to move beyond the superficial and get inside the reasoning so we are all more connected to the business and the customers. You know this has happened when your staff say things like, "Our customers", "Our business" and "Our culture" rather than the third person versions ("The business", "The customers" etc.).

> **Tip:** One of the key skills that future leaders will have is the ability to ask powerful questions.

—— ——

# Managing your time

## *Personal effectiveness*

Time management or personal effectiveness is an on-going skill to be learned. Even though we have heard lots of tips on this subject we still struggle to implement good practice. Everyone has exactly the same amount of time in a day. Yet some people always seem to be rushing about, behind schedule in their jobs and lives, while others are calm and unhurried and seem to get the same amount of work done in less time.

Avoid thinking that because you are busy, you are getting lots done. You need to allow some reflective thinking time to be effective. In fact, the more time you need to spend in your role thinking, reflecting and contemplating, the higher up the leadership ladder you're likely to be!

Time management will help you organise your time so that you are spending more time working on activities that matter and less time on activities that don't. It can help you become a more effective leader, and therefore more valuable to your employer and your team. It can also help you reduce your stress levels.

One thing you can do to identify where your time goes is to set up an activity log. This is where you record all your activities over a period of time (such as one week) and identify exactly what you spent your time on. This helps you accurately identify some of the time wasting activities.

Next, make a 'to do' list. This is a list of the important things you need to get done. Then prioritise this list. Identify what is important and what is urgent. Of course do the important and urgent things first. Try to avoid things becoming urgent as these activities are the ones that cause you to be under the most stress. If you can plan in advance, then you can avoid a lot of things becoming urgent and get them complete before they become so.

Set deadlines for things to be complete and allow a 'cushion deadline' which means you actually have some spare time in case of an unexpected interruption. Avoid making your deadline the same as the *actual* deadline.

## Grouping and interruptions

One technique that can save you time is to group similar activities together. If you have a few phone calls to make, schedule a time to make them one after the other and get into a 'groove' as you make the calls. If you are reviewing a report from a team member and you find an item that needs discussing, don't go to them immediately. Finish reading through the report and make notes on all items to discuss and do them together.

It's also important to manage your email responses. Consider turning off the email notifier and schedule specific times in the day to look at your emails. Unless your job requires you to answer every email immediately, plan times to read emails in batches. You'll find you have much more 'flow' going on in your work and that you are more proactive in your approach.

As a leader, you must be available for your team members when they need you. However, like any worker you need uninterrupted time to be able to get things done. If your door is always open, your team members will constantly be stopping by to ask you every little question that pops into their heads, and you won't have any uninterrupted time. The best way to balance your team members' need for your input and your own need for quiet time, is to set aside specific times when your door will be open, or walk around your team's area in the office at a particular time every day. You might also set aside a time when your door will always be closed. There will be urgent problems that team members have to interrupt you with, but you'll find that they interrupt you far less often if they know you'll be available for them at a particular time.

**Tip:** Avoid the trap of equating being busy with being productive. They often aren't the same thing.

# Running effective meetings

## *Key points*

Running effective meetings is part of the leader's role. We have all been in meetings that have dragged on, not met our expectation or had no real ending. Some meetings can be very frustrating, especially if there appears to be no purpose or that the original purpose is lost.

Be aware that it takes a really good meeting to be better than having no meeting at all. If you take this view, you will avoid having pointless meetings or meetings for the sake of it.

Have an agenda for meetings. Let people know in advance what the purpose of the meeting is and allow them time to prepare their thoughts and any contributions. This is especially important if people don't normally say much. It's probably because they need time to consider their thoughts. If you give them advance notice, they are much more likely to be ready to contribute. Set the expectation of the meeting so that people are on the same page. You can avoid disappointment by letting people know the purpose of the meeting.

For example, if someone is expecting a decision by the end of the meeting and you only intend to use the meeting as an opportunity to generate ideas, they are going to be deflated at the end as they have a different expectation to you. Help people to know what the meeting's purpose is.

During scheduled meetings such as a weekly team meeting, consider having a short training session. This doesn't need to be long, perhaps just ten minutes. Organise someone to present something as a training slot. It could be a refresher, something new, or a topic that you feel everyone could benefit from. This is one way to continue to develop your team on a regular basis.

Be an effective meeting manager by keeping control of what happens in the meeting. Don't let things go off topic too far unless you plan to. If a discussion starts to diverge off on a big tangent, consider using a 'parking lot' idea which could be a flipchart where you record the ideas to be discussed later.

Always complete a meeting with action points. A lot of people record minutes. These can be useful if you need an audit trail of what was discussed. Minutes are way more effective if you have SMART action points connected so you can measure the success of the meeting through action points assigned to relevant parties as a result. Allow the meetings to flow by avoiding putting people down that come up with ideas and thoughts of their own. Be respectful to them and encourage participation. You can limit participation by setting the expectation up front by saying something like, "We will only have time in this meeting to look at two or three ideas on the subject but we can table any additional ideas for a later meeting".

Start meetings on time. Don't punish the people who have turned up on time by waiting for those who are late. People will get the message quickly if you start when you say you will and also finish when you say you will. If you have trouble starting on time, consider putting a fun thing or important thing at the front so people won't want to miss out.

## Stand up meetings

If you want to ensure the meeting is short, try holding a meeting where everyone stands up – a stand up meeting if you will. No one wants to stand for too long, so call a meeting in a room without chairs and people will be less likely to ramble.

Keep the agenda short to accommodate the best attention and input from everyone.

## Walking meetings

A further variation in the creative meeting repertoire is to have a walking meeting. People seem to be far more comfortable walking than sitting in a meeting, plus you can get some fresh air. These work best if you have a pre-defined route so you don't waste time thinking of where to go during the meeting. Try to keep the agenda to one topic and you should see the ideas flow.

These meetings mean you don't worry about taking notes. They are more about engaging in deep conversation and exploring ideas. Keep the numbers of the meeting small – perhaps two to five otherwise you may have difficulty hearing everyone's views.

**Tip:**   Don't hold a meeting just for the sake of it. It takes a really good meeting to be better than no meeting at all.

— —

# Managing your boss

To some people, this topic may sound a bit suspicious. The phrase was coined in the early 1980s and has been a familiar catch cry in management circles to help subordinates find ways to develop a better understanding with their managers. Remember, this is about *managing* your boss not *manipulating* your boss, so these points are geared around helping you both have a better working relationship.

You may have mastered how to lead your team effectively but still struggle with your own boss. This is not uncommon and you are not alone. There will be times when you don't see eye to eye or when you feel like you are being dealt with unfairly. You may have unreasonable demands placed upon you or you may feel like you just don't click.

The first point here is for you to appreciate your boss's goals and pressures. Find out what they are measured on and what their 'pain' points are. If you can make them look good or ease their pressure, they will have more time for you.

One way you can view your boss is as you would view a customer. Find out what their expectations are and work to manage them. If your boss were a customer or client of yours, how would you handle that relationship? You would want to have regular meetings, inform them of changes, look to provide solutions and communicate effectively with them.

Never let bad news get to your boss before you have had a chance to brief them. If bad news is coming, you'd be much better off fronting up with the news yourself. Bad surprises are never good for your relationship. Provide frequent updates to your boss when a problem arises. If you have a problem, try to provide a solution or at least have some thoughts on the matter. Probably nine times out of ten, your boss will go with what you think is best.

Work out what is the best way to communicate with your boss. Do they prefer face-to-face, email or phone? Find out what they prefer in the way of reports and written communication. Do they like lots of detail or bullet points?

Tell your boss what you need. Be proactive in telling them your preferences and outline any resources you need to get the job done. Remember that you are not their sole focus, so try not to take all of their time.

Sometimes your manager will not be quick with decisions. You need to be able to communicate what you need in these circumstances. Help to sell the reasons as to why you need a decision when you do, and the downside of delays. Avoid sounding like the doom machine though. Don't make everything dramatic or imminent as your boss will quickly tire of that behaviour.

If your boss is about to make a poor decision, offer an alternative with some benefits attached. If they still proceed with what you perceive to be a bad move, do all you can to implement it, regardless of whether you agree with them or not. Do not undermine them in front of other people.

If your boss is vague or hesitant, limit the choices you give them and make a single clear recommendation. If you feel that things are vague, seek clarification to help you and them get clarity. Communicate your deadlines clearly and follow up.

If your boss is overly controlling or very involved in everything you do, it's likely that they need more confidence in you. Start off by asking for complete responsibility in smaller tasks and then work up to bigger ones. Prove to them you are quite capable. Make sure you deliver excellent work consistently and seek to build trust.

If your boss overloads you with work or fails to see what pressure you are under, organise a meeting to discuss the priorities and options for excessive work. Avoid sounding negative about what's asked of you and explain what problems may arise if you don't organise what's the most important priorities.

Overall, you want to be able to understand your boss and provide consistently good work. Help them to look good and be clear with them of your needs to.

Finally, make sure you keep your promises and do what is asked of you. One piece of management advice that will go a long way for you to impress those you report to is this: When your boss gives you three things to do; do at least four of them! This means that you should at least complete the tasks you have been given and perform an additional task. Something that you weren't specifically asked to do but you know either needs doing or would really help your boss if it was done. This will show you are resourceful and can take initiative.

**Tip:** Managing your boss is about making your working relationship better for *both* of you. It's not about manipulation.

— —

# Team charters

One way you can help your team to peer manage each other is to set up a team charter. This is a set of rules or guidelines that says, 'This is how we work around here'. You could include areas such as:

- Conduct towards each other
- Dress code
- What to do if you feel uncomfortable
- Work ethics
- What happens if someone is late for work
- How to show respect etc.

Always include the team in setting up a team charter. Never impose the guidelines and also consider what the consequences are for those who break the rules. You'll find that the team will self-police these guidelines if they are agreed upon and visible and that consequences are followed up on.

When new people join the team, the charter is something you can discuss at interview stage so that they understand what is expected in your team right from the outset.

There are many examples of team charters available on the internet. You can pick up some great ideas on how to get started. Consider canvassing your team's views on the idea and help them understand the benefits of having one. It's a great way to iron out some of the on-going niggles in a team and will help save a lot of your time resolving issues that won't even need to reach you.

—— ——

# Some final thoughts

As a leader, there are many aspects for you to put your energies into. Know that you will never know everything and there is always something to learn. No two situations are identical. No two staff members are the same. The more you know, the more techniques you develop, the better equipped you will be in dealing with your staff behaviours, leading them effectively and building the confidence necessary to be an excellent people leader.

Don't try to be a crowd pleaser. Trying to be popular will lose you the respect of your team members. In some ways, you need to ensure there is a little distance between you and them. If you need to pull someone aside and give them some developmental feedback, it's more difficult if you are a close friend.

Always follow through. The fastest way to build trust is to do what you say you will do. Ensure that you keep confidences and respect the views and opinions of others. Avoid speaking negatively of your superiors in front of your team members.

If something needs to be said, you should say it. Let your team know by your actions that you will deal with issues that arise. Be consistent in your approach so that everyone knows where they stand.

Have fun. Enjoy your opportunities to lead. You aren't likely to be 100% perfect in what you do, but try to be sincere and genuine and take the occasional risk and remember to communicate well to your team and show your appreciation to them. In short, be the kind of leader you would want to follow!

—— ——

# Other books available from Derek Good

Return on Investment Made Easy by Derek Good & Craig McFadyen

**Paperback:** 108 pages
**First Published:** July 30, 2010
**ISBN-10:** 1452835993
**ISBN-13:** 978-1452835990


Coaching and Feedback Made Easy by Derek Good

**Paperback:** 82 pages
**First Published:** December 23, 2010
**ISBN-10:** 1453844384
**ISBN-13:** 978-1453844380


ROI: The sales person's secret weapon by Derek Good

**Paperback:** 56 pages
**First Published:** August 24, 2011
**ISBN-10:** 1463764634
**ISBN-13:** 978-1463764630

Leading a Team by Derek Good

**Paperback:** 104 pages
**First published:** August 8, 2012
**ISBN-10:** 1478332034
**ISBN-13:** 978-1478332039

# Notes

Made in the USA
San Bernardino, CA
18 December 2019